LAST CALL FOR ALCOHOL

Healing a Marriage
Harmed by Alcohol Abuse

Susan Erling Martinez

tjsusan.com

Also by Susan Erling Martinez

*Angels & Dreams: Add Sparkle to your Life with the
Help of your Angels and your Dreams*

Life-Guard: A Woman's Personal Safety Guide

Safe & Sound: A Parent's Guide to Self-Protection for Kids
(Co-authored by E. Gordon Franks)

These books are available at www.tjsusan.com.

Susan's booklets on loss and grief are available at:
www.aplacetoremember.com and
www.wintergreenpress.com.

LAST CALL FOR ALCOHOL:
Healing a Marriage
Harmed by Alcohol Abuse

Published by: Tjsusan.com
7455 France Ave. S. #412
Edina, MN 55435

Cover design by TJ Martinez and Craig Dow

Edited by Amber Erling

Please Be Advised

This book contains the author's personal ideas for healing from addiction. It is not an accredited recovery program. Consult a chemical dependency counselor or facility for information on accredited recovery programs. The author and the publisher do not guarantee outcomes, nor accept responsibility for the results of suggestions made in this book.

DEDICATION

*This book is dedicated with enormous love to
my parents, Jack and Nora Borden;
without their example
I would never have known that true love,
between a husband and a wife,
was really possible.
May your reunion in heaven
be as blessed as your union on earth!*

TABLE OF CONTENTS

HIGHER POWER

Higher Power, Mighty Star
How I wonder who You are.
Up above us all so high
Like an Icon in the sky.

What on earth were You thinking
When You gave me a man who loves drinking?
Were all my good deeds forgotten
Or was my karma all that rotten?

Higher Power, Mighty Star
Sometimes I wonder *where* You are.
Why have You left me stranded here
With a man who loves me less than beer?

Susan Erling Martinez

PREFACE

Once there was a little girl who was raised to hate alcoholics. And when she grew up, she married one.

This is a story about a marriage that never should have happened, lasted, or triumphed. It contains all the elements found in an R-rated movie: sex, violence, crime, rampant addiction, out-of-control emotions, a colorful Latin hero, a spirited blonde heroine, a villain name Lord Alcohol, and dazzling angels.

It's my story. If it were made into a movie, Antonio Banderas and Cameron Diaz might be playing the lead roles. Or maybe Lucy and Desi...

Alcohol was an unwelcome guest in my home for six years, like a parasite that attempted to suck the life out of us. But my husband and I--with help from some friends in High Places--stopped it.

This book is based on actual events and real people. I haven't even changed the names to protect the innocent. It's not a fairy tale, not a flimsy romance novel, not a recovery book. *Last Call for Alcohol* is the culmination of experience and experiments. It offers my ideas and suggestions for recovering from the harmful effects of another person's alcoholism, and for living a healthier, alcohol-free lifestyle.

If you find peace, joy, healing, or any other positive results from trying one or more of the suggestions, then we all win. I like to think of *Last Call for Alcohol* as a spiritual adventure, which is how I also like to think of my life, so far.

It's funny to me how we end up doing things we swore we'd never do, in my case, writing a book about recovering from alcohol abuse when I don't even drink alcohol. Even in my hungriest days as a writer, you couldn't pay me to write about this topic. Then one day, I knew I *had* to write a book about this subject, even though I am not a professional or expert in this field. My expertise lies in personal experience and contemplation.

In this book, I describe my scary adventure through the sunless streets of fear, self-doubt, and delusion, and my emergence into the sweet valley of sanity, sobriety, and true relationship with my mate.

It's about being fully human and fully spiritual; about resurrecting the dead, namely a dead or dying sense of Self. It's about transforming your suffering into something peaceful, joyful, and beautiful; and about having a loving, playful, alcohol-free marriage in a world that adores and often needs alcohol. Sober doesn't mean dull and boring. It's about beating improbable odds, and becoming a torch-bearer for others walking or staggering down the dark, twisted path called Addiction Alley.

So far, I admit that my life has been a somewhat bumpy, but interesting ride. Understanding my husband's horrendous disease has made me love, understand, and not be so quick to judge people. I learned to forgive human frailties, even my own.

Through it all, I believe that I evolved as a human being. Yes, I may have grown up hating alcoholics, but I ended up deeply loving one. This is our true love story. May your story also have a happy, hopeful ending. And like the lotus, may you grow sweetly even in the muddiest waters.

Susan Martinez
Edina, Minnesota
October 2001

INTRODUCTION

Before I begin this tale, I'd like to share with you a bit of information about alcoholism, and how it effects those afflicted with the disease and their loved ones.

Alcoholism is the third leading cause of death in the United States today, and it runs in families. Most health care experts consider alcoholism a disease, and not a character defect or weakness. Many think it's an allergic reaction to alcohol. Its chief symptom is the overwhelming compulsion to drink alcohol, in spite of the horrendously negative consequences to self, family, and society.

Untreated alcoholism will eventually result in insanity or death. No lie. And even though it affects millions of everyday people, the true cause and the real cure are still not fully known or understood.

The recovery statistics are disparaging.

~Only 15 to 25 percent of alcoholics recover. Of those 75-85 percent who don't obtain permanent sobriety, 25 percent will eventually kill themselves.
~Alcoholics Anonymous has only a 12 percent recovery rate.
~80 to 90 percent of people treated for alcoholism relapse, even after they have sustained years of abstinence.

Alcoholism: Does heredity or overindulgence cause it? That question is still up for debate. All the experts know for certain is that abstaining from using alcohol seems to be the key to recovery.

Alcohol is a cruel taskmaster. It mercilessly abuses its victims, and these victims, in turn, victimize the people they claim to love. Fitness guru and recovering alcoholic, Susan Powter, wrote in her book, *Sober...and Staying that Way*, "Alcoholics don't abuse alcohol; alcohol abuses them." I agree.

Like secondhand smoking, which kills 53,000 people per year, secondhand alcoholism (my name for it) negatively affects and "kills" unsuspecting people, who are in close proximity to the addict. I was exposed to alcoholism as a child (both of my grandfathers were alcoholics), and later as the wife of an alcoholic.

11

Secondhand alcoholism is a health risk for everyone in relationship with an alcoholic--wives, husbands, mothers, fathers, children, siblings, friends, co-workers, everyone. Scientific evidence shows that excessive alcohol consumption is most hazardous to the drinkers themselves. However, there is compelling evidence that regular exposure to an active alcoholic threatens the safety and health of people near the drinker.

Symptoms of secondhand alcoholism include feeling unsafe, unloved, and unworthy, and being at a greater than normal risk for domestic violence, health problems, depression, addiction, accidents, suicide, and murder. Children are especially vulnerable to secondhand alcoholism, and have a greater risk of becoming alcoholic themselves compared to children from non-alcoholic families.

Here are a few more cold statistics:
~In 60 percent of child abuse cases, alcohol is involved.
~In 40 percent of rape cases, alcohol is involved.
~In 65 percent of reported fatal accidents, alcohol is involved.
~In 80 percent of suicides, alcohol is involved.

And the list goes on. Of course, statistics mean little unless you're one of them.

In his book, *Overcoming Addictions: The Spiritual Solution*, Deepak Chopra states, "Alcoholic beverages can be thought of as drinks, but they can also be defined as drugs. In fact, alcohol is by far the most abused drug in the United States. One important study proposes that alcohol accounts for 85 percent of America's total drug addiction problem."

Alcohol is an easily obtainable drug, and it's cheap. Most children can get it free of charge right from their parent's own liquor cabinet. Then these same parents are shocked to discover that their children are full-blown addicts by age sixteen.

Without repercussion or remorse, liquor dealers and bartenders legally supply would-be and hopeless addicts with their daily fix. In fact, barkeeps are rewarded (tipped) for pouring extra powerful drinks. Beer manufacturers use wise-cracking amphibians, sexy couples, and celebrities to tempt and program young people into believing that alcohol consumption is harmless and necessary in order to make friends, have fun, or get easy sex.

I would describe my life with an active alcoholic as living inside a bottle. When you're in a close relationship with an alcoholic, try as we might, us mere humans somehow end up climbing inside the bottle with the addict. I don't mean to imply that we start drinking, too, but we enter the bottle just the same.

So why did you go inside the bottle?

You may have slipped into this invisible prison cell created by the addict while you were innocently chasing after love. You may have gone in willingly out of a sense of obligation to a sick family member. You may have been sucked in by empty promises. You may have gone in--hissing and swearing--against your better judgment. You may have even been forced inside against your will.

I went in because I thought I could save the addict. But in the end, it doesn't really matter how you got in there. What matters is that once you're inside the hopeless, bottle-like world of the alcoholic, you're stuck in there, like a model ship built by an ambitious hobbyist. It may look pretty from the outside, but inside the bottle, all is dead and stinking.

I found that living inside a bottle was suffocating, like living in a see-through coffin. You watch the world go by from behind glass. You can feel yourself decaying like a corpse, but you don't know how to stop it. I have come to believe that this is the closest one will ever come to being in the mythical state of hell.

Living inside a bottle separated me from reality, from my true Self, and from other people who loved me. Living inside a bottle was also hazardous to my health and to my sanity. The only message that I found in that bottle was: "Woman, get out now!"

Eventually I was forced by harsh experiences to see that existing inside a bottle with an active alcoholic was incompatible with life. I was dying in there, like a captured butterfly. Then an angel came to me in a dream, erasing all fear, and infusing me with the love, the power, and the will to get out. And I did.

Getting out of the bottle is very difficult, but very necessary if you want to live. It's at least as difficult as getting off alcohol or drugs, I think. Getting acclimated to life outside the bottle can be very difficult as well, but also very necessary. *Last Call for Alcohol* is the story of how I got out of the bottle *without divorcing my mate*. My hope is that my experience and success will coax you out, too.

Mental health professionals tend to label people like me, and maybe like you, "co-dependents." But I am not fond of that label, or diagnosis.

I'm not exactly sure why I never could tolerate the term *co-dependent*, especially when it applied to me. I didn't think I was co-dependent, although many people wanted to stick that tag on me. I didn't whine, nag, stomp my feet, or wail "Woe is me!" Well, hardly ever.

I wasn't sick, he was. I wasn't a victim. I didn't dig taking care of and trying to control others. I didn't lie to protect him, but I did (and still would) lie to protect my children. I just happened to be married to an alcoholic.

As time went on, I wasn't trying to save him as much as I was trying to save myself. I didn't neglect my own survival in order to take care of overly needy people. I'm not a Mother Teresa.

Adapting to your surroundings, even if they're negative, is an innate survival mechanism found in all sentient beings. Sunflowers turn towards the wonderful sun. Turtles tuck in their heads when danger is present. And the loved ones of addicts adapt. I am convinced that if we didn't adapt to our circumstances, we would be as unhealthy as the addict. How we adapt is up for debate.

In her book, *Codependent No More*, Melody Beattie writes: "Codepedents aren't crazier or sicker than alcoholics. But, they hurt as much or more. They haven't cornered the market on agony, but they have gone through their pain without the anesthetizing effects of alcohol or other drugs, or the other high states achieved by people with compulsive disorders. And the pain that comes from loving someone who's in trouble can be profound."

This explanation was somewhat more palatable to me: I hurt at least as much as he did. I found it interesting that whenever I said out loud that I wasn't co-dependent, someone would invariably say, "You're in denial." Why is someone always in denial if they don't come up with the same conclusion about themselves that others do? Since I couldn't win, I didn't say it. I don't even like saying it here.

Perhaps "interdependent" is the better word. We are all dependent on each other in various ways.

1
WHAT THE LITTLE GIRL SAW

HOW CHILDREN ARE AFFECTED BY ALCOHOLISM

I don't remember ever not knowing that my grandfathers were both drinkers. All of the terrible stories that I heard about their drunken escapades, compounded by their obvious failure to provide properly for their families, cast gloomy shadows upon my pristine child-mind.

To me, they were worse than the most horrid monsters imaginable; worse because they were real monsters, created no doubt by the poison they drank. Growing up, I believed them to be weak, selfish, and heartless people.

I was born in 1953, the third child, the only daughter. My mother always said that I was her fondest dream come true. My first awareness of alcohol came at a very young age. I was about three years old when I first heard about drunks. On numerous occasions, I would overhear my parents hotly discussing one or both of my grandfathers.

Patrick, my fiery Irish maternal grandfather, was infamous for getting loaded, and chasing my poor, fat grandmother through the backyard, swearing and throwing empty soda bottles at her, while their ten children looked on. Not only did he possess a thirst for Irish whiskey, but also was the proud owner of a sizable Irish temper. I still remember his rumpled clothing, unshaven face, deep violet eyes, and his wonderful Irish brogue. He was notorious for his rambunctious, drunken, cussing poker games on Sunday nights.

Thomas, my tormented paternal grandfather, drank in Hemingway-esque style. I recall his jazzy piano playing, haunting writings, emotional outbursts, and the smell of booze on his breath. My dad once told me this story about his father:

"Everyday when I was walking home after school with my friends, we would see my dad walking home from the store, carrying a shopping bag. Inside

16

the bag was his daily dose of alcohol--a six-pack of beer and a bottle of wine. I was so ashamed when my school friends saw him, because I knew that they all knew what he had in the bag."

Tears flooded Dad's 79-year-old eyes when he added, "I never loved him." My heart lurched with compassion. If he didn't love his father, he wouldn't cry, I decided.

I also noticed as the years went on how other family members were added to this tipsy group, including aunts, uncles, and cousins. The grisly details about how these poor relatives trashed their lives, and the lives of their spouses and children, were often the topic of conversation at the family dinner table.

Mom, it seemed, was always tolerant of our very crazy family members. But, Dad wasn't. He hated alcoholics and lived in fear that he would someday become an alcoholic like his father. To prevent a similar tragedy, he carefully rationed his beer intake, allowing himself to partake in only one beer a day. No more. Seldom less. I believe he lived his whole life afraid he might become like his dear old dad.

On weekends, my parents would save their relatives. They would ride in from the comfy suburbs, like modern day saviors in their white Chevy, to their homes in the housing projects or inner city. Mom and Dad brought them food, medicines, and whatever else they needed.

I watched from a distance, politely detached, as my parents cleaned their parents' dirty, smelly homes, including discarding used toilet paper that was tossed on the bathroom floor instead of the in the toilet. I looked on in utter disgust as my mom and dad picked their mothers, fathers, sisters, brothers, nieces, and nephews off the floor, both literally and figuratively. Even at a tender age, I saw how futile it was to offer counsel, time, money, prayers, energy, and love to people who refused to help themselves. My heart hardened.

I also saw that divorce, illegitimate children, poverty, and criminal activity were also common occurrences in those strange realms just East of sobriety. Without being told out right, I knew that all this heartache, chaos, and drama was caused by alcohol.

In spite of my wacky relatives, I grew up quite nicely in a middle-class, very functional home. My parents, Nora and Jack, were lively, funny, and ferociously in love with each other and us kids. I was their golden child, small, blonde, intuitive, artistic, and pampered. My brothers, Garry, Jack Jr., and Ted, were the opposite, loud, dark-haired, and wildly bursting with life. We were a spicy mix, us Bordens.

Except for my alcoholic relatives, my childhood was altogether perfect. I thought of those poor souls as black ink blotches on the pretty pink canvas of my life. They made me feel afraid and ashamed, and in my young heart, I never felt love, or compassion for them.

At some point in my life, I don't exactly remember when, I began to think of alcohol as a creature that I named Lord Alcohol. He was the monster that lived under my bed. This dragon-like thing was a gigantic green reptile with lion's claws, a serpent's tail, great wings, and slimy, scaly skin. Of course, he breathed fire when suitably provoked.

Every night, Lord Alcohol prowled the earth, seeking to snatch the free will from poor unsuspecting souls. To hide his true identity, he would shape-shift into fruity wines and potent cocktails. By morning, he owned many souls. Some victims, no doubt, were easier to own than others. Some, I imagined, were like hot wax beneath his mighty seal ring, while others probably tried to spar with him. I thought that Lord Alcohol was as deceptive and wicked as the Black Widow spider who seeks a mate, courts him, seduces him, then bites his head off.

As a child, I knew that I was safe from Lord Alcohol as long as I didn't let my small hands drop off the mattress and get too near his hideout under my pink and white, canopied bed. As a grown-up, I knew I was safe from him as long as I didn't drink his deadly nectar.

I often thought that Lord Alcohol's evil twin was Puff the Magic Dragon. Throughout the course of history, this legendary pair, alcohol and marijuana, has had amazing success keeping the whole world anaesthetized and addicted. I still can't help but wonder when, oh when; will the people slay these dragons?

When I was in Catholic elementary school, I learned about Prohibition in history class. During the period from 1920 to 1933, the 18th Amendment was in force, making the manufacture, transportation, and sale of intoxicating liquors illegal. My dad was born in 1920, and no doubt his own father had quite a time obtaining alcohol for those "dry years." I heard rumors that he drank rubbing alcohol and bathtub gin. When I was a child, I liked the idea of Prohibition, even though the majority of Americans during that era did not. I could see in a rather Zen-like way what many adults could not; that alcohol is harmful to people, to families, and to society.

When I was six years old, my dad's brother, Dick, was killed in a car accident. He was only twenty-eight years old. Dick's friend was driving. He was also drinking and speeding. My mom was seven months pregnant at that time with my youngest brother, Ted. Dick's death was a huge family tragedy.

I remember being at my dad's side at the funeral when he approached Dick's friend, and loudly berated him for his carelessness and stupidity. It was a mortifying experience. The suffering in the room was as thick as smoke. I'm positive that many sorrows were drowned that night, and many nights to follow with many tall drinks.

By the time I was eleven, all four of my grandparents had died. The men died from the effects of excessive alcohol ingestion and smoking. The women died of broken hearts, I think. Their bodies may have died, but their legends have not. Their memories cast eerie shadows far, far into the future. Some days I still stand in their cool shadows...and shiver.

Shortly after their deaths, I began writing poetry. These poems, I was told, were not the ramblings of an innocent child's mind. Rather, they were a young girl's penetrating look at the early 60's. I wrote about the Viet Nam War, the flower children, racism, social injustice, spiritual mysteries, hunger, far and away future loves, the raping of Mother Nature, and of a God, who dabbled in people's lives like a nosy neighbor. I was told that my poems rattled the nuns who taught me in school. But I think they also intrigued them.

The indisputable fact that Grandpa Thomas was a gifted writer was another unsettling fact. When I was just a budding writer, I feared that I too might become an alcoholic like him someday. I remembered reading how Marilyn Monroe greatly feared mental illness, because her mother was mentally ill. To dull this burgeoning fear, she drank and popped pills, which probably made her mentally ill...and dead. Was it her fear or her genes that caused her to follow the family blueprint? Who really knows?

I wondered if I would become a great writer or great guzzler. Time would tell.

2
FIRST CALL TO ALCOHOL

1969

TAKING THAT FIRST DRINK

My first taste of alcohol came at age fifteen. In was 1969; the summer of Woodstock, a man on the moon, and meeting the man I would marry a few years later. My girlfriend, Jeannie, and I had snuck two cans of beer from our folks, and gulped them down like Kool-aid, even though they tasted ghastly. The beers made us feel reckless, invincible, and terribly funny.

I thought I was God! Then in an ethanol haze, I decided to drive us around the neighborhood in my white Corvair convertible without a driver's license or a stitch of sober sense. Swerving, speeding, laughing, and unabashedly alive. The wind was in my face, in my hair, and blowing through the holes in my head.

My rational mind knew it was a decidedly stupid thing to do, but my chemically altered mind loved it. Honestly, I don't think I have ever had as much exhilarating fun since!

Drinking alcohol for the first time is like losing your virginity. It stings at first, floods your body with heat; then it explodes in your head. From then on, you crave it. The upside was that we didn't get hurt or caught. The downside was that I got violently ill. As a result, I have never drunk another beer since. To this day, the smell of beer still makes me nauseous. So that was my first beer and my last. Needless to say, my lesson was learned early on.

I think that most kids take their first drink of alcohol, either because of peer pressure or curiosity. They also might try it if they see their parents have a drink each night to relax. A child may think that this is normal behavior, which it is in many families. If Mom and Dad do it, it can't be bad.

Although I have drunk alcohol on occasion in the thirty plus years that followed that first beer, I have lived a comparatively alcohol-free lifestyle. I drank more than usual in my late thirties, during my divorce, but I never really liked the way alcohol affected me. It made me so silly, so bold, and so reckless. It made ordinary men look like gods and dull people terribly amusing. It distorted reality too much, and usually made me sick even after just one glass. Publicly, I attributed my aversion to booze to my devotion to Buddhist teachings. Privately, I blamed it on my contempt for alcoholics.

3
FATEFULLY YOURS

1993

CHOOSING AN ADDICTED MATE

By the time I was thirty-nine years old, I had been married for twenty years, and given birth to five children, including a set of twins. I had three pregnancy losses, had my son Jake diagnosed with cystic fibrosis and diabetes, wrote two self-help books, earned a black belt in karate, lost my younger brother Ted in a car/train crash, co-founded a non-profit organization, and got divorced. Someone once told me that I had lived five lifetimes in the span of those four decades.

As the Big 4-0 loomed, I was having a ball; single, dating, and happy. My five kids were ages 11-19 at that time, and as a family, we were as thick as thieves. I was working at that time as a free-lance writer and press agent. My life was really quite entertaining.

In early 1993, I met an unusual man named TJ Martinez at Gatlin's, a country nightclub in the now world-famous Mall of America. He was the club's disc jockey and country line dance teacher. Gatlin's was a magical place; a place where your craziest dreams could become your even crazier reality. It was easy to become addicted to Gatlin's. Just take a sip and you're hooked.

The ritual at the club was the same every night at closing. It's 12:45am. The patrons, who have been line dancing and drinking for five or six hours, are by now fueled by liquor, ignited by the music, and smoldering with sexual tension. Then suddenly TJ would "pause" the music for a moment and then announce: "Last call for alcohol!" Groans and curses would quickly rise up from the loud and loaded patrons and stick to the smoke-stained ceiling, as they rushed en masse towards the closest liquor supplier for a refill. It never once failed to surprise me how this four-word announcement always bothered the "regulars."

Their groans would coax a memory to the surface of my subconscious mind. I'm six years old, and my cranky teacher has just announced that recess is over. I groan, stamp one foot down hard, and know the bitter truth: No more recess. No more fun. Shoot!

Then at 1:00am the music stops for the night, and TJ would add, "Ladies and Gentlemen, please return your dates to their upright position. Drink your drinks and head for the door." More school kid groans. It's time to stop drinking, dancing, and prowling. Time to go home. Time to re-enter reality. Shit!

At Gatlin's, everybody loved TJ. He had a cocky confidence, a world-class wit, street smarts, and a distinct musical sense. He personally knew many famous recording artists, which added to his mystique. Beneath the brim of his cowboy hat I saw eyes as black as sin, and a face that told a thousand stories. He had long black hair, olive-skin, and was more exotic than classically handsome. And, damn, he could dance! TJ was cool before it was cool to be Latin. But he wasn't my type.

TJ boasts that he fell in love with me on first sight. He says that he saw me dancing and told his buddy that I was his future wife. How arrogant was that? Well, it just so happened that his buddy was dating my girlfriend, Debbie, who sang in the house band. To give credit where it is due, I would never have even gone to Gatlin's in the first place if Debbie hadn't worked there and insisted that I go hear her sing. And even though I hated country music at that time, I went to Gatlin's a few times to see Debbie perform, and to dance with the cute yuppie cowboys.

So TJ--not being of sound mind--decided to have Craig ask Debbie to set he and I up on a blind date, which she did. However, when I later found out who my blind date was, I was truthfully horrified. "Oh, God, not him! I won't go! I can't stand that guy!" I loudly complained to Debbie, but she insisted that I keep my word. (Debbie had this way of *insisting* things.) However, after listening to me bitch about it for a week, she had mercy on me, and eventually told TJ that I didn't want to go out with him. I was so relieved.

The first time TJ Martinez ever spoke a word to me was when he approached me in the club and offered to let me out of the date.

23

"You don't have to go out with me," he said quietly. I could tell he was highly uncomfortable, standing there before me, shameless with infatuation.

"I said I'd go and I'll go," I thoughtlessly blurted out. His face fell. I knew I hurt his feelings, but so what? After all, I was doing him a big favor by going out with him. Then I felt guilty for being so mean. To balance the nasty karma, I quickly gave him my telephone number. Six weeks later I finally kept my word and agreed to meet TJ at Gatlin's on his night off for our infamous not-so-blind date.

But things did not go I as had imagined they would. They went how they were destined to go.

To my utter surprise that first date was like one of those romantic black and white movies. Gatlin's was uncharacteristically empty that night. We sat at a table for two and chatted, mostly about Gatlin's gossip. I drank that night, but he didn't, which now seems highly ironic.

As we talked, I could feel my apprehensions quickly fading. I was starting to like the guy. He was sweet and kind and even shy, quite the opposite of his brash and sarcastic disc jockey persona. Then the song "Desperado" by the Eagles beckoned us to the deserted dance floor. Answering the call, TJ took me by the hand, led me to the center of the floor where the spotlight lives, tugged me to his chest, and then began to slowly sway with me.

The song's lyrics sent a wild chill up my spine. "Desperado, why don't you come to your senses? You've been out riding fences for so long now. Freedom, oh, freedom, well, that's just some people talking. Your prison is walking through this world all alone..." Silently, I wondered if the lyrics were about him or about me.

Then something must have tickled a tender spot in my heart, sending the most sublime sensation through my chest. Love? I felt weak and strong. Intoxicated. Everything around us became diffused. The only clear thing from my perspective was TJ--his firm torso pressed against mine, his arms circling my body like a halo, his animalistic rhythm, those black eyes, and that mouth. Then it happened. Like an irresistible prince from a fairy tale, the man kissed my lips and changed the course of my life forever. Love! After that night, we were inseparable.

To me, TJ was like the night--dark, mysterious, and thrilling. And, to him, I was like the morning--open, mystical, and promising. When we came together, boundaries blurred, things, once clear, appeared gray. We were exact opposites and totally alike. We were like yin and yang incarnate.

Love was too common a word for the emotion that burned between us. It was bliss and it was blasphemy, and when we were together, all that mattered was he and I. This instant love, we intuitively decided, must certainly be leftover from previous lifetimes with each other.

We soon became dance partners, performing nationwide in clubs and in Diane Horner country line dance instructional videos. Our lives quickly became entwined, like partners performing a sultry dance, pure energy, momentum, and passion.

When the idea of marriage entered my conscious mind, I asked God for His opinion. That night I had this dream: TJ was going from house to house in our town, asking women to try on this glass cowboy boot. But no one could fit into the boot. When he offered the boot to me, my foot slipped easily inside. Shouts of joy rose up from the town people. When I awoke, I knew I had finally found my "cowboy prince."

TJ proposed to me in showy style on my fortieth birthday, and I married him in a western-style wedding on the Gatlin's stage after knowing him only seven months. In the weeks before the wedding, I worried about many things. Mostly, I worried about how my five children would handle having a stepfather. They hated the idea, of course, which darkened my joy. This, I knew, would be a marriage born of fire.

I also had quite a time deciding whether or not to legally assume his last name, Martinez. It was just too ethnic, I decided, especially when worn by a green-eyed blonde of European descent. The name would never fit the face. The kids and I would have different last names. I would be an official member of a Mexican clan that I barely knew. However, in the final cliff-hanging moments before the nuptials, I did decide to accept the name he offered me and wear it proudly.

Oh, the wedding! I wore a saucy late-1800's style white hat, a white western wedding dress trimmed in silver thread and fringe, and white cowboy boots with silver-studded toes. TJ wore a pure white cowboy hat, western-cut tuxedo, silver

25

LAST CALL FOR ALCOHOL

bolo, cowboy boots, and spurs. The large ballroom vibrated with unbridled energy, music, guests, and promise.

My brother, Reverend Jack, was the marriage celebrant. Before the wedding he confided to me, "I'll marry you this second time, but not a third." Fair warning.

I had to choke back tears when I saw my father, sweet mother, and five children decked out in their western gear and nervous smiles. The only thing that blemished this pretty picture was my knowing how much my children wanted me to be married to their own father, not to TJ.

When I walked down the aisle, escorted by my dad and then seventeen-year-old son, Jake, the song, "Love of a Lifetime" by Firehouse, permeated the room like an aphrodisiac for ears. I certainly felt like the fairest of them all.

The local news media got a kick out of covering the story: the author and the cowboy. I must admit that we were quite a dazzling pair! Unfortunately, our sparkle quickly dimmed.

If I had had my third eye open, I might have seen a very ominous sign of things to come. Barely one week after the wedding, a Gatlin's waitress dumped a tray full of drinks on TJ's pure white wedding cowboy hat. The pungent liquid poured down the brim and into his lap. He swore. The waitress cried. And his prized wedding hat, as dear to him as my wedding ring was to me, was utterly and permanently ruined by the alcohol. In retrospect, I should have seen this as a warning signal. But I didn't.

4
ON THE LIP OF INSANITY

1994-1996

LIFE WITH AN ALCOHOLIC

A few months after the wedding, the bare, naked truth--that TJ was a certifiable alcoholic--emerged. Two drinks a night turned into twelve. Two lovers turned into sparring partners. Two months together felt like dog years.

I felt so stupid and embarrassed when I realized that I had married a man who was already married to the bottle. I had married that which I hated: an alcoholic. And just as the metaphysicians had preached, I had drawn to me what I feared the most.

In the *Dhammapada*, the Buddha said, "And the man who engages in the drinking of intoxicants, right here in this world, he digs up his own root." During the next six years, I would witness TJ's uprooting and the hideous effects of his twenty-eight years of daily alcohol consumption.

He told me that he started drinking out of his father's liquor cabinet at age thirteen and never stopped. He also admitted to smoking, snorting, and popping a smorgasbord of drugs, but never injected any.

When he was sober, TJ was a charming, incredible man. There was nothing mundane about my husband. His favorite line when he entered our house was to call out in his Ricky Ricardo accent, "Lucy, I'm home!" Not a day went by when he didn't have me rocking with laughter or smoldering with sexual fire.

But when he drank, he was mean and mouthy. His verbal attacks were devastating. No one in my life had ever spoken to me with such malicious words. Remember that I was the golden child raised on praise and love, never spanked or whipped with devastating words.

27

I don't know if his drinking escalated after we got married or if he just stopped trying to hide it from me. Maybe the roles of good husband and stepfather just didn't suit him, further exacerbating his illness.

In 1994, just nine months after our wedding day, he was arrested for taking a swing at me when I tried to take his car keys away from him during one drunken episode. Although he never hit me, he was jailed overnight, convicted of fifth degree assault, and fined.

I was so stupefied by the whole scenario that it never occurred to me to leave my new husband. In retrospect, this was the moment that I think I slipped inside the bottle with him, totally certain that big-strong-me could save him from Lord Alcohol and from himself.

In 1995, we separated briefly. The chaos was killing me. However, just one month after we had reunited, he was arrested for Driving While Intoxicated (DWI). I later found out that this was his 3rd DWI since 1988.

He went to court, to jail for a week, lost his driver's license for a year, and went into an outpatient chemical dependency treatment program. I hoped that he would get sober. I even tried a few Al-Anon meetings, but didn't especially like them. I wanted to talk about him, him, him, but they would only let me talk about me, me, me.

By that time, TJ had already been fired from three good disc jockey jobs for drinking on the job. His chemical dependency counselor suggested that he should stop working in bars and start a new career, so he went back to college for a year.

I was beginning to believe that being married to an alcoholic was like cohabiting with a cobra. Dangerous.

In 1996, just eleven months later, he got his fourth DWI, plus he was driving without a driver's license. He went to jail overnight, and at my request, my parents bailed him out. The repercussions of this arrest were loud and expensive. Our only car was impounded in accordance with state law. There were many court appearances, more fines, two more years without a driver's license, but no jail time because the arresting officer had screwed up.

As the wife of a "repeat offender" I was forced to have special license plates on my car, which announced to the world that the owner of this car had multiple alcohol-related driving offenses. Since I was the only one of the owners who had a valid driver's license, I drove around for years, wearing those "drunk plates" like a scarlet A.

Sometimes idle cops would pull me over for no other reason than to check for alcohol and drug use. I was mortified, lamely telling them that I followed Buddhist teachings and didn't even drink. It crushed my sense of pride to read the same question in their eyes: *Why are you with him?* All I could do was shrug. Many times strangers would notice my "drunk plates" and ask me about *my* DWIs, but I was generally too ashamed to tell them the truth.

Meanwhile, TJ was ordered by the court to attend to a chemical dependency relapse program at the famed Hazelden Center in Center City, Minnesota. Knowing the great reputation of this spendy facility, I had high hopes for TJ's recovery. However, my hopes quickly fell when I found out what really impressed him most about Hazelden was their gourmet food, not their recovery program.

Did he stop drinking? No. He drank more.

5
LOSING MY INSPIRATION

1997-1999

LOSING YOUR ROLE MODEL

In 1997, my best friend and beloved mother, Nora Borden, died. She was only seventy-two years old. My mother was on her deathbed, skeleton-thin and coughing, for thirty days. Although she had never been a smoker, she developed pulmonary fibrosis, a lung disease that scarred her lungs, and eventually suffocated the life out of her. It was a gut-wrenching experience to witness the cruelty of such a death. Pain is one thing, but not being able to draw a breath is worse by far, in my opinion. If you've ever seen someone die of lung disease, I don't think too many people would choose to smoke cigarettes. It was insufferable.

Mother's Day, 1997, was a surreal day, one of those days that you know you'll never, ever forget. It was the day of my mother's wake. That day I wore a dress I knew she'd like. I made sure that all five kids and both husbands (present and past) would attend. I gathered my ghastly emotions together, metaphorically wrapped them in a nice, clean handkerchief, and tucked them away in my purse, so no one would see them. Pandora's purse.

On my knees at the foot of my bed, I prayed potent, frightening, delirious prayers. *God, take this crap away from me! Jesus, wake me from this nightmare! Mom, come back to life! Mom, take me with you!* Then, in creepy silence, I rode with my family to the Mother's Day activities, held that year at a funeral home.

I don't remember walking in, but I do remember seeing her, lying there in her casket, like a beautiful wax doll in a display box. She was wearing the pretty pink dress that I had bought her. How she loved pink! Flowers rose like anthems all around her. So she was mortal after all, I sadly realized.

My brother, Reverend Jack, pointed out that mom had a little smile on her lips. I bristled. That's not a smile, I shouted inside. It's the shape the lips take before a person screams! The funeral director gave me Mom's three diamond-studded rings in a little blue velvet pouch. I didn't want the damn rings. I just wanted her back.

So, on that strange Mother's Day in 1997, all the people came to look at her and to hug us. Everyone wept. Everyone, except me. Wasn't I the one who easily blubbered, watching the suffering of strangers on the nightly news? So why didn't I cry for my own mother? Without my tears, I must have looked cold and uncaring. Damn. Where did I leave those tears? Oh, yes, in my purse.

A wake must make one awake. I mean it. This really happened to me.

I drove home from the wake alone after TJ thoughtlessly decided to attend a Ringo Starr concert instead of coming home with me. As you can imagine, I was quite down and out with the sickening odor of embalming fluid clinging to my clothes. Then it happened.

About a mile from home, suddenly everything around me changed and appeared surreal. The tires didn't seem to touch the road, yet my car moved along quite normally. The road before me waved like a black ribbon from a funeral bouquet. The trees and shrubbery that lined the road slowly undulated, pulsing up and down. The glorious pink and blue sky up ahead met the road and melded with it. And for a moment, I too waved and undulated, pulsed and melded with everything around me.

The steering wheel was part of my hands. My right foot and the gas pedal kissed and merged. My body and the car seat pressed into one another, warm and willing, like intergalactic lovers. My mind knew such sweetness. My heart fluttered with ineffable joy. And my soul danced like a mischievous sprite across my dashboard. Oh, my!

This, I later decided, must have been what the mystics have called the ecstatic state, where All is One and One is All. *Satori*. Somehow--perhaps it was a gift from my mother--I had pierced the veil between the material and the spiritual worlds. It lasted for maybe a minute, and then it was gone. And I turned back into a pumpkin. Rather, I turned back into a bereaved daughter.

When I got home, I collapsed on my bed and cried my broken heart out. Apparently a gallon of tears had slipped out of my purse when I wasn't looking. To this day, I have not totally forgiven TJ for leaving me alone after the wake to attend that stupid concert. How insensitive can one human be? He came home sloshed, of course. But I was too drained to fight with him.

Losing your mother changes you at a core level. You intuitively know that you will never be the same again. You also know that no one will ever love you like that again in this lifetime. Nothing in life could have prepared me for such a monumental loss. Today, I am still reeling from its effects.

By the end of 1997, TJ had quit college and started a new career in banking. This time, he didn't drink on the job, although I found out, after the fact, that he drank a half-pint bottle of rum every night after work at his bus stop in downtown Minneapolis. Then he took a bus home. I also discovered that alcoholism was as common as a cold in his family, although most family members were now in recovery.

In the morning after a drunken episode, TJ was always cheerful and loving, remembering none of the incident or his verbal abuse. His amnesia was too convenient, I thought, and my memory was too long and clear.

TJ's alcoholism wounded me in places where fists, knives, or bullets cannot reach. He wounded my spirit. I loved him. I hated him. I wished he were dead. I wished I were dead. I didn't want to live with him or without him. Moreover, he crushed my sense of trust, self-respect, and optimism. Dead Woman Walking, that's how I felt.

I wrote this poem during one of my many lows.

Husband. Husband.
I have spread my arms wide open for you.
And my reluctant thighs.
I have spread open the scars on my heart to let you inside.
I have spread wide open my mind, hoping to catch a wisp of understanding.
I have spread my love thickly upon you, like rich frosting on a cake.
Yet every bite I take tastes more bitter than the last.
I have spread myself so thinly that I fear I have become invisible.
All that I am now is an unfinished poem.
A message never spread.
A teardrop lying in a shadow, created without light.

Why didn't I leave him? There were many simple and complex reasons.

I stayed because I loved him and had entered a sacred covenant with him. In my thinking, he was a sick family member, which made staying with him seem like the loving and compassionate thing to do. In our society, it's considered heroic to stay with a spouse with cancer, but idiotic to stay with a spouse with alcoholism. Go figure.

I stayed because I believed in miracles. I really believed that someday he would be miraculously healed.

I stayed because I believed in reincarnation and karma. I knew in my soul that he and I were here together, in this time and place, for a very important reason. I believed that we had come together to fulfill a pre-incarnation promise to be together and to neutralize some lopsided karma.

Author Melody Beattie writes this about karma in her book, *Playing It by Heart*: "Karma means you're seated, strapped in, and along for the ride--even and especially when the ride turns into something different than you thought it promised to be."

If I left, nothing would be accomplished, and we'd have to try again in another life. If I stayed, there was hope that he and I could be healed and freed from our karmic conundrum.

I also stayed because I felt that leaving would be weak, and that dish was worse, I thought, than the plate that was already in front of me. I didn't appreciate weakness, especially in myself. I must also state here that I would have left if there had been physical abuse, or even a threat of physical abuse. No one is safe staying with an active alcoholic who is violent. I never felt in danger physically.

Why did you stay?

Every year I would get a psychic reading, each time from a different psychic in various parts of the country. Secretly, I wanted the reader to declare that TJ was the wrong man for me, and insist that I leave him. But, inevitably, the psychic would say, "Stay with him and work it out. He is your soul mate. He is your twin soul." I would leave each reading knowing that I should stay with him, but also knowing that I should leave him. So for the next long year, I would sit on the proverbial fence, cursing my fate.

In 1998 we celebrated our five-year anniversary. TJ sweetly said to me, "These have been the best five years of my life." In my mind I said, "These have been the worst five years of my life." The worst part of those years was his lies.

Both 1998 and 1999 were more years of high drama, blackouts, missing money, prescription drugs for alcoholism that never worked, useless A.A. meetings, hypnotherapy, visits to sacred healing sites, vitamin therapy, plus my bouts of depression and major abdominal surgery.

Desperation is not a pretty sight. At one point, I was so desperate that I offered to buy him a Harley-Davidson motorcycle if he would get and stay sober. To own a Harley had been TJ's dream since he was seventeen years old, but judging by his bland response, that dream was not as great as his desire to drink.

Once I called the paramedics because I thought he had overdosed. It was a false alarm, but I was highly disturbed when the emergency technician asked me, "How long has he been abusing you?" I snapped back, "He doesn't abuse me!" Then I struck the formidable pose of Xena, the Warrior Princess, and added, "I'm a black belt. I can take care of myself." But later that night, I knew the horrible truth: TJ had been abusing me verbally, emotionally, and psychologically for nearly six years.

At that point, I asked his family would participate in an intervention, but they regretfully declined. Anger and questions rose up in me like scorching lava. I blamed his family for appearing to be so indifferent. Never in my life had I ever felt so alone and so utterly pitiful. Not even the beloved poet, Rumi, could comfort me. My life sucked big time.

What helped to keep me going? I would have died--literally--without daily prayer and meditation. Other significant factors were my deep love for TJ; my five grown kids, who still needed a sane and happy mother; my parents who believed me capable of miracles; my companion angel, Mariah; great books by visionary authors, my wise girlfriend, Jamie; and my unflinching friendship with God. All my life, I have been buoyed by angels and blessed abundantly. I always felt that I was indisputably one of the lucky ones, although my luck seemed to be running out.

6
THE MILLENNIUM'S END

1999

HITTING ROCK BOTTOM

Shortly before Christmas, 1999, TJ came down with what I thought was a terrible virus. I actually thought he was dying. Later I would find out he had alcohol poisoning.

Being born on Christmas Eve, TJ naturally loved Christmas time, and it showed. He over-bought presents for me, and thoroughly enjoyed every traditional aspect of the season. On Christmas day we visited his relatives at his parent's home. But by the time I was ready to leave after five hours of visiting, TJ was drunk and obnoxious. Apparently, he had been sneaking the Christmas cheer. Moreover, he refused to come home with me.

So there I was, home alone on Christmas night, while he got inebriated in the name of family togetherness. He was the Grinch who stole my Christmas, a real ass-hole. When he called me at midnight, we fought bitterly. I hung up the phone angrier than I had ever been in my whole life. Not merely angry, but enraged.

"Do something drastic!" my soul screamed out.

And so I did. Shaking with rage, I dropped hard to my knees, pressed my white-knuckled fists to my chest, focused my crying eyes on the ceiling, and demanded like a mad tyrant, "God, heal TJ now! God, heal me now! I'll accept nothing else!"

The impassioned demand was so fierce that I frightened myself. Nervously, I waited for lightening to strike. It didn't. A moment later, I began to feel a strange tingling sensation at the crown of my head; the kind of goose-bumpy feeling you get when you experience something reality-defying, like a very odd coincidence, deja vu, or a ghostly visit.

Looking back, I believe that at that moment, I popped the cork with my pain and passion, and then burst like a long-trapped genie out of the bottle I had been living in with TJ. I was free. I was mad. And I was out for revenge.

So while TJ slept in his parent's basement on an old couch, and I cried and cursed myself to sleep that unholy Christmas night, I believe that the spirits convened to plot their rescue attempt.

That night I had this Big Dream: I was slated to fight the karate champion of the world. I felt completely unprepared, as I hadn't sparred in many years. I tried to back out of the fight, but my girlfriend Jamie, who was my manager, gave me a pep talk.

"Susan, you've got to fight one more time. You still have what it takes to win this match."

"Jamie, I can't do it," I insisted. "I'm too tired. I have lost my warrior spirit." Jamie wasn't deterred.

"Just one more round. Pretend it's just an exhibition, not a real fight."

All I could say was, "I can't do it. I'm too tired."

Then as I turned to leave the scene, I was stopped by Ricky Martin, the Latin singing star. He smiled into my soul, held me close, and then with thought transfer, told me that I was strong, beautiful, and capable. I felt enveloped in his divinity. When I looked at his face, I saw that he glowed. Even the blonde streaks in his hair glistened. Immediately, I realized that this was an angel in disguise, and I fell instantly in love with him.

I don't remember fighting the fight, but I do remember waking up feeling as if I had won it. What was the message of this dream? I had to fight one more match, which I assumed it meant one more round fighting TJ, the pecker-head, and Lord Alcohol. To this day, the memory of Ricky, the nocturnal angel, has never faded from my memory. When I think of him, I feel strong, beautiful, and capable. Later that morning TJ called. He was remorseful, but I was not forgiving. I didn't want him any longer. I wanted Angel Ricky.

I begrudgingly picked TJ up later that day, and watched in disbelief as he took his drugs to treat alcoholism, and washed the pills down with Bailey's Irish

Cream and coffee. The ride home was Minnesota-cold and quiet. He wasn't worth fighting for any longer, I decided. I wanted things he couldn't give to me. I wanted peace. I wanted normalcy. I wanted true, real, unbreakable love. Later that night, he promised to stop drinking for good on January 1, 2000. I pretended to believe him, but I didn't.

New Year's Eve 2000 was a strange night. I had caught the Y2K bug, and was quite concerned about the impending midnight hour. Meanwhile, TJ drank a whole bottle of champagne, and finished off a bottle of Bailey's Irish Cream. As always, he was soon drunk and mean. We argued and he called me a "dumb bitch." My warrior energy detonated, and I was instantly transformed into a fire-breathing she-monster. Honestly, I was so furious that I had to literally sit on my hands to keep from pounding him with my fists...but I am not proud to admit that. As always, TJ had ruined another fine occasion with his drinking.

Oddly enough, he wore a tee shirt that night with the slogan "YOU AND WHAT ARMY." It was as if he were taunting me subliminally, "You and what army is going to stop me from drinking?"

Morning dawned. All was quiet on the home front. TJ turned to me in bed and said, "I drank my last drink last night. My days as a career drinker are over. I'm done now." I pretended to believe him, but I didn't. He also reminded me that I had promised to buy him a Harley if he got sober. I hadn't forgotten my desperate promise. "The promise is still good," I said.

That first day went fine. No hint of booze was anywhere. The next morning TJ awoke from a Big Dream. He said, "In my dream I was locked in jail with this other guy. I was being jailed for things that I hadn't done. In order to get out, I had to tell the authorities that this other guy was the guilty person, not me. So I snitched big time on this guy, and he yelled, and swore, and threatened me. Then I was let out of jail. I was free."

I was emotionally overcome by the significance of that healing dream. The dragon, Lord Alcohol, that had held him hostage for twenty-eight years, had finally released him. Now TJ was out of the bottle, too.

After that dream, TJ no longer craved alcohol. He said that the desire to drink was "lifted from him." He had an epiphany of the highest order. A true miracle had happened. It humbled me to witness the power of a real spiritual awakening.

7
ON THE WAGON

January 2000

GETTING AND STAYING SOBER

It was a grueling journey to the Land of Sobriety. When we arrived, my husband and I seemed like the survivors of a major catastrophe, objectively observing the state of our lives, as if we were viewing our homeland after a level-four tornado had hit. We were in shambles, like demolished houses, but for the first time in many years, we had hope. It was time to heal. It was time to build a new house.

The first week he detoxified physically. He had night sweats, his hands shook, and he emitted toxins on his breath. His forty-one-year-old body had found a way to cope with continual alcohol consumption, and now it was finding a way to manage without it. I imagined that his poor liver was undoubtedly grateful.

The first week I glowed with joy and gratitude. I couldn't believe that the nightmare was finally over. It was as if everything about our life together had changed overnight. My husband didn't drink, and the primary source of our conflicts suddenly disappeared. TJ happily attended A.A. meetings three times per week, got a sponsor, and attended mass on Sundays; something he hadn't done in more than twenty years. He tried to make amends to his family, his friends, and me, and desperately hoped I would forgive him and let the past go.

He got his driver's license reinstated after five years without one, and ordered a Harley-Davidson motorcycle, which he fondly referred to as his "highest power." He read the A.A. Big Book cover to cover, and then read it once again. He showed compassion for others who suffered, regret for past misdeeds, and was certain that he was cured. He was becoming a better man.

But so much change so rapidly made me dizzy. I found myself often saying, "I feel overwhelmed!" Being in that state of drastic change reminded me of when I was a new martial arts student, and my instructor was attempting to teach me how to do a jump spin wheel kick. The object was to jump off the ground with both feet, spin around 360 degrees, and end up clobbering an opponent in the head with the side of the foot.

Change feels like that: off the ground, spinning in mid air, and aiming at some invisible target. If you miss, you land hard on your ass. If you're too slow, your opponent strikes at you first, and you land hard on your ass. Sounds a lot like real life.

The change in TJ was undeniably dramatic. There were new lights in his black eyes, like tiny stars twinkling in a midnight sky. He was filled with exuberant energy, and often wore me out with his ideas, adventures, and excitement for living. He even exhausted our two cats out, wanting to play games with them. When he was still drinking, he never thought he could have fun without being drunk, or at least tipsy. Now he was proving his theory highly false. Where he once believed, "Rehab is for quitters!" he now believed the profound words of the Serenity Prayer. He even told jokes about alcoholics, and bragged about his recovery to everyone.

I watched this all transpire before my eyes, while in a state of incomparable shock. If my eyes were any wider my eyeballs would have fallen out, and rolled onto the floor. The first month of his sobriety was indeed quite confusing to me. I apparently didn't know the rules of this new sober game. How should I act? What should I say? Is my stinking thinking shrinking? Moreover, I didn't want to do anything that might pop this magnificent bubble that surrounded us.

During the hush of midnight, sometimes I'd lie awake and seriously wonder if TJ was a Walk-In. In her ground-breaking book, *Strangers Among Us*, Ruth Montgomery describes this paranormal phenomenon: "A Walk-in is a high-minded entity who is permitted to take over the body of another human being who wishes to depart...The motivation for a Walk-in is humanitarian. He returns to a physical being in order to help others..." Apparently, the spirit that previously inhabited that body proceeds into the spirit realm for rest and contemplation, before embarking upon another physical lifetime. Who is this man in my bed?

Many husbands and wives innocently assume that their marriage will be problem-free once everyone is sober. I know I did. But they often find that, although it's immeasurably improved and workable, it's loaded with problems that they never knew existed. Like us, they may find themselves feeling alienated in a world that adores alcohol, out of place in the heart of society after living on the fringes so long, or feeling very uncomfortable without their coping mechanisms (alcohol, denial, rage, control, victim-hood, etc).

I was inundated with turbulent emotions and thoughts: fear, anger, sadness, confusion, a sense of betrayal, distrust, guilt, regret, vulnerability, and everything in between and beyond. The enormity of the emotions was deeply disturbing, rattling me to my bones, and forcing me to feel and experience them. After all the effort and energy I had spent learning how to squelch such potent emotions, suddenly my emotional boiling pot was gushing all over the place, and I couldn't slop the contents back inside me. I had inadvertently lifted the lid on my Pandora's box, and all the ills of my world ran out. I cried easily and often. I was on fire inside.

Country artist Martina McBride's hit song, "Love's The Only House," has a great line in the chorus. It goes "the pain's got to go somewhere." These words struck a resounding chord deep within me. If the pain and suffering has got to go somewhere, where might that somewhere be? I had no idea.

8

THE NAKED TRUTH ABOUT SUFFERING

February 2000

STILL HURTING AFTER YOUR MATE IS SOBER

Even if I were a drinker, I don't think wine could console me during the second month. I was in a state of unadulterated suffering.

To be a human being is to suffer. Buddha said so. Even in our brightest moments, a bit of pain hovers darkly about the edges. I think suffering begins for most of us at birth. Not so much from the physical discomfort or the sudden separation from mother, but when the soul inside that baby body realizes: "Oh, no! I've incarnated again! What was I thinking?" Now, that's what I call suffering.

Suffering is a state of anguish, deep anxiety, unspeakable misery, intense sorrow, or abject hopelessness, caused by what the person perceives to be a great loss. Suffering can manifest to varying degrees as physical, mental, emotional, or spiritual pain, or all of the above. I even think that the word "suffering" is insufferable.

A few years ago, Linda McCartney died of breast cancer. When the press asked her husband, ex-Beatle Paul McCartney, how he was doing, he answered, "I am totally heartbroken." His words broke my heart, as I imagined his utter devastation at the loss of his darling mate. Apparently, no man or woman is immune from pain and suffering. Money can't prevent it; nor can fame, power, religion, or position.

If I had the cure for suffering, I'd take it myself, and then give it to everyone else free of charge. But I don't. I think that the one thing that can end or at least lessen suffering is having an unshakable knowing that suffering is a temporary condition.

Wise, old Solomon said, "To everything there is a season, and a time to every purpose under the heavens..." The seasons of suffering will pass either with or without my cooperation. I'll either get happy or sick or insane or dead. Ultimately, I choose the outcome. Suffering stops eventually. Nothing lasts forever. Not the good times, nor the bad. Not the full moon, nor the full blooms. Nothing lasts forever, except perhaps some bad memories.

The Buddha, the prophet formerly known as Siddhartha Gautama, was raised as a pampered prince in a kingdom near Nepal in India about 2500 years ago. After his enlightenment, he devoted his life to the understanding and elimination of suffering. His teachings on suffering are referred to as The Four Nobel Truths. These Truths are the foundation of the Buddha's teaching:

1. Life is full of suffering.
2. Desire is the cause of suffering.
3. There is a way out of suffering.
4. The way out of suffering is following the Eightfold Path.

Let me try to explain. The first truth states that human life includes suffering. He said that birth, illness, aging, and death prove that suffering is synonymous with life. Although there seems to be a million different causes for suffering, the Buddha affirmed that there is just one cause.

The second truth explains the cause of suffering. He stated that suffering occurs as a result of desire, or wishing circumstances were other than they actually are. It's being *attached* to an idea that people or things should be other than how they really are. It's a state of *non-acceptance*. Alcoholics, especially, are experts at non-acceptance. This compels them to change their awareness of themselves and their perception of the world with booze. Others do it with drugs, food, cigarettes, gambling, and shopping, to name a few.

The third truth is that it is possible to be free of suffering. The good news is that freedom from suffering (craving, attachment, and non-acceptance) is possible. No one has to suffer, unless he or she chooses it.

The fourth truth states that this freedom from suffering comes about through right, present-moment living, as described in the Noble Eightfold Path:

1. Right Views
2. Right Aspiration
3. Right Speech
4. Right Conduct
5. Right Occupation

6. Right Effort
7. Right Attention
8. Right Concentration

I think that the first time I truly experienced a state of true suffering was when my fourth child Jesse was stillborn. I was twenty-eight-years old at the time. I refused to accept his sudden death, and spent many difficult years wishing that things had turned out differently. Even when my twins were born a year later, I still grieved for Jesse. I had nightmares for six years about his birth, relieved only by hypnosis.

I know now that I was living in a suspended state of non-acceptance, and consequently suffered intensely. Yes, the source of the pain was real and undeniable--the death of a baby--but I exacerbated the pain by fighting it, by trying to push my way through a jet stream. I vowed to be more accepting and bendable in the future.

My brother's and my mom's deaths caused me to suffer, as did my divorce, and later TJ's alcoholism. Sometimes I felt that Fate was not my friend, but that didn't prevent me from trying to cultivate acceptance and present-moment being.

Even if I had a crystal ball, I don't think I could've predicted what was going to happen next, or how soon I would be forced to test my newfound attitude about suffering. Just six weeks into our recovery, we received a telephone call at 11:00pm from my brother Garry's wife, Cathy.

"I've got bad news," she tentatively said. "Dad's dead."

"No-ooo," I softly cried out. Adrenaline flooded my system, and I could physically feel my heart contracting, like a labor pain in my chest. "Dad died," I mumbled out in disbelief to my husband. Spontaneously, TJ wrapped his arms around me. "What happened?" I asked her. "God, what happened?"

My father, Jack Borden, was found dead in his home of an apparent heart attack. He was seventy-nine years old and in good health. Adding to the tragedy was the fact that he had lied there dead on the floor for 24 to 30 hours before his body was discovered. He had been living in an Assisted Living apartment administered by the city of St. Paul. My brothers and I had hired the staff to check on Dad each morning, and if he ever missed a meal in the cafeteria.

Although he had missed all three meals that day, no one investigated. Could he have been saved if they had done their job right? Maybe yes. Maybe no.

Grief, guilt, anger, sadness, and unanswerable questions stormed the fortress of my mind. Why this? Why him? Why now? Why me? Fate, stop tempting me!

I tried to console myself with the thought that he and Mom, who had been loving mates for fifty-plus years on earth, were finally reunited in Heaven. It had been god-awful to watch him try to live without her for nearly three years. When Mom died, I felt sorry for Dad. When Dad died, I felt sorry for myself. I decided that there is no right or easy time to lose your parents. You always need them, even when it seems as if they have little or nothing left to give. Now I faced a new challenge: mid-life orphan-hood.

Losing both parents is like suddenly having home plate removed from the Game of Life. Now where are you supposed to run to? I sometimes wonder if they will come back together as my grandchildren, or as my parents again in another lifetime. I hope so.

I also drew a bit of comfort knowing that my dad had achieved his most cherished goal: he never became an alcoholic like his father. He proved that even genetically predisposed people, like him and like me, don't have to be powerless over alcohol. In reality, he was closer to a saint than a sinner. He was my mentor, my friend, and the president of my fan club. He was bigger than life...and bigger than even his own death.

I quickly decided that being in mourning was like being in hell, hell without the bells. Being in mourning was like being mad, as mad as a hornet in a shoebox. Being in mourning makes you destructively creative: You try and try to create ways to make the whole f---ing thing just not so. But it is so. TJ's Serenity prayer began to speak to me in the night. It said over and over: "God, grant me the serenity to accept the things I cannot change..." Things like my dad's death. And even though Dad's leaving rocked my world, this time TJ was there for me in every way.

God, I certainly had my work cut out for me as I embarked on my process of healing from the effects of secondhand alcoholism, compounded by my father's recent death. Still, I vowed to accept *what is*, which meant I would first have to accept *what was* (the past).

In order to accept *what was*, I had to honestly name it and claim it. I married a sick man. The truth was that no one forced me into the marriage. I could've left at any time. I stayed because I chose to. In choosing to stay, I either consciously or unconsciously chose to accept the karma or ramifications of my choice. I wasn't a victim. This new outlook was pivotal and essential to my personal recovery, and to the resurrection of our relationship. Without it, we would be unable to move on and become well.

Next, I had to fully see and accept *what is*. What is the nature of things at this moment? Mom and Dad were dead, making me by default the new matriarch of the family. My kids were great: Amber taught ballet, Jake managed a clothing store, Noelle was in college, and the twins were juniors in high school. Our careers were going well. TJ's recovery was going great. Money was no problem. A big concern was that my health was not great, mostly stomach and abdominal problems, which I understand is common in loved ones of alcoholics.

However, my biggest concern was that I didn't trust my husband. I could forgive him, but I couldn't trust him not to drink again. Alcoholics lie about everything. From their perspective, they have to lie in order to survive. I didn't know how trust happens. Is it earned or given? I was never an untrusting or suspicious person before I met TJ, but now I was. Trust would undoubtedly be my greatest block to surmount.

So that is *what is*. I really saw for the first time the sheer elegance of accepting *what is* even, and especially, when *what is* is unacceptable. Not necessarily liking it, but accepting it, nonetheless, because that was the high-minded thing to do, the thing that would bring about peace and healing more quickly. I vowed to cultivate an attitude of acceptance. But first I would need to heal the wounds. But how do I do it?

Once again the words to Martina's song came to mind, gently wafting through my mind like an angels tender whisper. "The pain's got to go somewhere..."

9
EXORCIZING THE DEMONS

March 2000

HEALING YOUR BODY, MIND, AND SPIRIT WITH PRAYER, MEDITATION, AND WALKING

By the third month of recovery, I knew I could no longer store the pain in my body, as it was causing great disharmony in my guts. The day my father died, my doctor had diagnosed a mass in my abdomen. I would later learn that it was not cancerous, but may require surgery someday. I had already had nine surgeries in the past, and one more may prove to be one too many, according to my doctor. I had to find another way to heal.

Highly desperate, I decided to perform an exorcism, of sorts, of my pain. If I couldn't let it go, I would make it go. In Roman Catholic and Pentecostal churches, exorcism is a rite used for the expulsion of so-called evil spirits. Once, I witnessed an actual exorcism on a three-year-old boy, and it was powerfully and permanently effective. The apparently possessed boy had spoken in four separate voices, besides his own, and growled like a wolf if he were brought in a church, or shown holy objects. The exorcism was performed while he and his mother were under hypnosis, and now ten years later, the young man is quite normal and unencumbered by invasive supernatural forces.

Although I didn't think that I was possessed by evil spirits per se, I was inundated with unhealthy thoughts, emotions, and memories. These were my demons. My goal was to make peace with them, shake hands, and send them on their way. And I vowed to do whatever it took to accomplish my goal.

I have come to believe through experience and observation that the illusive cure for any addiction, including secondhand alcoholism, is willingness. One drop of undiluted willingness to become clean, sober, healthy, and free is the secret ingredient to curing addictions. When the addicted person is ready and willing, the cure will come. When I asked TJ why it took him so long to stop drinking, he said, "I wasn't done yet. I wasn't ready." Moreover, he wasn't willing to be well.

Any recovery plan will work if it is preceded by willingness. But how is "ready and willing" instilled in an addicted, or even a non-addicted person? That's the million-dollar question. All I knew for certain was that I was ready and willing to become well, whole, happy, and free from suffering.

Peace, I believe, is the opposite of suffering. And peace, or freedom from pain, is what humans deeply crave, which is why so many people turn to their addictions for relief. I firmly believe that it is possible to alter your consciousness without using a drug or other addictive substances or activities. I use what I call my free detoxifiers: prayer, meditation, and walking.

These three precious jewels have the power to take you to that sweet place that exists between the material and the spirit worlds. This magical place, sometimes called "the gap" is where all things physical are manifested. In the gap, my soul lives, the spirits live, your dreams live, and God lives. Every human being goes to the gap every day, during daydreams and night dreams, while making love, or simply spacing out. But some people go there on purpose and at will. These gap-goers are the magical people, the mystics, and the enlightened ones.

PRAYER

Prayer opens a portal to the gap. But there appears to be no one sure-fire way to pray. Some people like traditional prayers that they recite again and again, like mantras. Some like to send their prayers to God via intermediaries, like priests, shamans, and angels. Some like to pray in churches, in groups, or outside in a natural setting. Some use prayer wheels, rosaries, rattles, OMs, or hymnals. Some people pray in pews posed like the praying mantis. And some people, embittered that their prayers are never answered, don't pray at all.

I love to pray. Prayer is my direct link to God. I pray or commune with God every day, all day long. I pray for guidance, insight, strength, patience, love, hope, joy, healing, and courage. I pray constantly for the safety and well being of my five children. I pray for those who need it, and for those who think they don't. I pray for stranded drivers on the side of the road, for hungry people everywhere, for children in need, for women who cry, and for grieving people. But mostly, I pray that God never gets tired of hearing my prayers.

Without prayer, I would be desperately lost and alone. Praying is like breathing. Once you start, you come to life. Once you stop, you die. Praying is an exorcism. It casts out evil spirits, which are also known as negative thoughts and disturbing emotions. Praying is like drinking. You get high on spirits without a hangover or DWI. Praying is like falling in love. You glimpse God. You flirt. You talk. You make love. You pull back. Then you return and unite in spirit, forever and ever. Prayer is my drug of choice. It disperses the pain and provides a beautiful escape from the troubles of everyday life. The more I use; the better I become.

In *The Alchemy of Prayer*, author Terry Lynn Taylor further explains the benefits of praying: "Prayer is actually therapy. When you pray, you are engaging in a psychic process of healing, and exercising the skill to solve problems with your inner wisdom. You are also programming your mind to look for positive solutions and to calm down and *respond* wisely to life instead of overreacting to situations."

The first formal prayer I ever learned was the "Hail Mary." I thought of it as an ode to womankind. It evoked and infused me with the strong, feminine Goddess energy, and comforted me on many a long, lonely night. Still does.

"Hail Mary" was my mom's favorite prayer. This is my version: *Hail Mom, full of grace. God/Goddess is with you. Blessed are you among women and blessed is the fruit of your womb: me. Amen.*

So I began to pray with new passion. *May I be happy. May I be free of suffering. May I be healed. May I forgive those who have harmed me. May I trust even where trust has been broken. May I be guided. May I be open to change. May I love and serve others. May I be at peace and bring peace to the world.*

At the end of each prayer, I would offer my troublesome energy to the Universe to be transmuted and used for the good of others. Never underestimate the power of a good, heated discussion with God.

My life still was far from dull even with all of my conscious intentions to find peace. It seemed as if every day something else would come up to challenge me to be more, be better, and become whole. During this month, TJ decided to quit his nice, secure job at the bank, and go work for his father's aerial mapping business. It seemed as if he suddenly couldn't get enough of his family. His dad owned the flourishing company and his brother was his boss. His uncle, sister-in-law, and nephew were also co-workers. This new job meant we would have to move into a home closer to his work.

I was surprised to see how easy it was to tip me off kilter. Just the idea of a new job and the prospect of moving again quickly sent me into a harrowing tailspin. Those overwhelmed feelings that I experienced so often during the first month of recovery flooded back. The red warning flag flew up and I knew I had to do something fast. "Meditate!" the voice of an angel inside me shouted. I had been meditating since 1988, and knew it worked, so I dove headlong into longer, more regular sessions.

MEDITATION

Like prayer, meditation also opens the portal to the gap, that magical place where miracles are made. When you're open, good things can come into you and not-so-good things can go out of you.

Meditation is easy to do, too. Just sit down. Be quiet. Breathe deeply and focus on each breath, nothing else. After a while, you'll feel centered, peaceful, and even unaware of your physical body. Be there fully for as long as you can. Then return to the world. Daily mediation is sublime. It puts you in direct contact with your own sweet soul, and the Creative Source. Your ability to manifest what you want happens quickly from that state of consciousness.

But knowing it and doing it are two different things. Sometimes, I just felt too nuts to meditate. Sometimes I felt that if I were any lower, I'd be underground. On days like that, when I was in the greatest mental and emotional anguish, the last thing I wanted to do was to sit and meditate.

What I really *wanted* to do was scream like a banshee, foretelling my own death, run a dozen red lights, get desperately drunk, run down the street naked with my hair on fire, or fling myself face first into a mud hole. But what I really *needed* to do, more than anything else, was just sit in silence. For down in the center of me, I knew was the peace that I desperately craved. For twelve years, I have meditated, so not knowing what else to do, I would go to my sitting spot, sit down, and close my eyes.

At first, I would feel as if I was sitting in the middle of a ghastly tornado. My shitty thoughts would fly around me like shingles that were yanked off roof tops by the merciless winds of Fate. Some of the shingles whiz by and narrowly miss me. Others hit their mark, slapping me across the face and laughing as they spun away. And I would sit there, feeling like a damn fool, and wishing I were anywhere, but there. Even digging up flowers at my father's grave, I decided, was better than that.

I sat. I breathed. I sat. I breathed.

Then, I would start to feel my body sink deeper into my cushion as I relaxed and let my weight down fully. My breathing would become slower and deeper.

My turbulent thoughts would begin to run out of steam. It was working.

Soon I started to sink deeper into myself. Down there somewhere, beneath all my layers of junk, I knew lied a mother lode of peace. Down I would go. Drifting. Drifting. Sinking like a smooth pebble dropped in a fishpond. And there it is. Ah, sweet, orgasmic peace. I felt like a jubilant miner who finally hit pay dirt!

Alive in my peace, I would pretend that I was a great Zen Master, serene, wise, and compassionate. In my open right palm sits Jesus; in the left, the Buddha, and in the center of my heart is the Goddess. And they are all smiling. The union is ecstatic. Then from out of the blue, a lovely little line from a Rumi poem touches my mind like a kiss. It goes, "Dance, when you're broken open..."And with such a beautiful thought now on my mind, I happily return to full consciousness.

Meditation teacher, Sharon Salzburg, writes in her book, *Loving-Kindness: The Revolutionary Art of Happiness*, "Sometimes we take quite a journey-- physically or mentally or emotionally--when the very love and happiness we want so much can be found by just sitting down." So I sit down and I breathe and then I can go on.

At the end of each meditation session, I thanked the wise men and women from the East who brought meditation to the West. Caspar, Melchior, and Baththazar may have brought the infant Jesus gifts of gold, frankincense, and myrrh, but their descendants undoubtedly gave humanity the gift of meditation. Mentally, I sent them all a blessing like a kite into the clear sky with a wee ribbon of my pain tied to the tail.

WALKING

The benefits of walking for fitness are well known and documented. All you need is a pair of feet and walking shoes. Some experts believe that walking is the quintessential form of exercise and stress reliever for the masses. But did you know that simple walking has the potential of also leading you through the portal into the gap?

Since I retired from practicing the martial arts, I have walked to ensure my sanity and to pacify my vanity. It wasn't intentionally meant to be a sacred or healing activity, just exercise. At that time, I was oblivious to the bounty that Mother Earth was offering all around me. She has the power to heal us, and we, in turn, have the power to heal her. It's a beautiful give-and-take that I failed to notice most of my life.

There have been many great people who have really walked this Earth. Jesus walked the hills and deserts of Palestine, teaching and healing those who suffered. The Buddha walked the endless terrain of India, teaching others how to heal themselves. Ghandi and Martin Luther King, Jr., the prophets of nonviolent resistance, held peace marches or walks. Peace Pilgrim, a wise, old woman, walked across America for twenty-eight years to promote inner and global peace. I also greatly admire one other saintly person in modern times who promotes walking for inner peace. He is Thich Nhat Hahn.

Thich Nhat Hahn is a Vietnamese poet, Zen master, Buddhist monk, and peace activist. Martin Luther King, Jr, nominated him for the Nobel Peace Prize. At his home in Plum Village, a retreat community in southwestern France, he teaches the art of mindful living and walking meditation.

In his book, *The Long Road to Joy*, he describes walking meditation: "Walking meditation is meditation while walking. We walk slowly, in a relaxed way, keeping a light smile on our lips. When we practice this way, we feel deeply at ease, and our steps are those of the most secure person on Earth. All our sorrows and anxieties drop away, and peace and joy fill our hearts. Anyone can do it. It takes only a little time, a little mindfulness, and the wish to be happy."

This gentle monk also advocates conscious breathing and using healing words and phrases with each step you take, such as "I have arrived" on the in-breath and "I am home" on the out-breath. He also suggests that you wear a little smile when you walk.

I started my walking meditation in March just as the Minnesota snow and ice was vanishing. Since I lived in a beautiful, safe area, I could walk on the sidewalk around my home, on the walking trails, to the grocery store or the library, or through the park. In nasty weather, I could walk inside the nearby shopping mall with the other "mall walkers."

My first attempt at walking meditation was awkward. My muscles felt tight, and the cars, people, blisters, insects, and ten thousand intrusive thoughts easily distracted me. Like an uncoordinated dancer, I was out of step. Sometimes I felt worse after my walk instead of better, but in retrospect, I think that was because I was stirring up and releasing toxins and negative energy.

But soon I got the hang of it. My movements became in sync with my breathing, which I knew was a sign of forthcoming proficiency. I was getting it. When I walked I focused on my feet meeting the ground one at a time, on my breath as it easily moved in and out of my body; and on my mantras, which I created anew every day.

Sometimes on the in-breath, I like to say or think, "God Is." Then on the out-breath, I think or say, "I Am." Depending on my mood or need, I might say or think, "I am happy" and "I am peaceful" "I am open" and "I am free" or maybe "I am alive" and "I am grateful."

Every day I would walk, allowing the pain to seep through the soles of my feet and into the Great Mother. On most days, my walking meditation lasted only thirty minutes, but its benefits were astounding. I felt lighter, as if I could walk on air like Tinkerbell. The heavy burden that I had carried in the hollows of my body felt less dense and dark. The thick slab of grief that surrounded my heart thinned. Sometimes I felt emotionless and thoughtless. I was just feet, breath, and God.

Thich Nhat Hahn writes, "When the baby Buddha was born, he took seven steps, and a lotus flower appeared under each step. When you practice walking meditation, you can do the same."

I really loved that idea, so I began to envision flowers beneath my feet and one tucked behind one ear. I filled my house with flowers, blessed the little wild flowers that I met on my walks, and saw myself as a lotus flower, blooming even in muddy waters. Often I could feel my companion angel, Mariah, and even my parents walking beside, commenting on the scenery, praising the wonders of God, giving advice, and expressing their love for me.

You can't go wrong if you lean on prayer, meditation, and walking.

10
THE LIONESS WITHIN

April 2000

RECLAIMING YOUR SENSE OF SELF

April in Minnesota is an unpredictable time of year. Mother Nature can't decide if she wants to snow or rain, hail or shine, create floods or droughts. If the Great Mother can't make up her mind, what hope is there for me?

I was really missing my mother at that time. I knew she would be so happy to see TJ finally in recovery. His alcoholism, and all that it entailed, was like a thorn bush growing in Mom's lovely family garden. One time she candidly admitted to me: "I would never be able to stay with him, if it were me. I just couldn't go through it. I worry about you constantly. I cry about your situation every day." Shortly after that, her pulmonary fibrosis began to squeeze the breath out of her. I knew she died worried about me, and that knowing still makes me very, very sad.

Then one day out of the deep blue, something happened. Suddenly, I had the urge to roar, to declare my womanhood. I became fixated with finding and reclaiming what Lord Alcohol had stolen from me. What was lost, I determined, was my lioness spirit.

Being exposed to alcoholism for an extended period of time commonly produces a feeling of being fragmented, or even empty. I knew at age forty-six that I was not the same woman I was at age forty, before I met and married my husband, and before my parents died. That woman was strong, brave, happy, healthy, and animated. She was up for any challenge, willing and able to fight for righteousness. Although I was getting somewhat better, I still felt like a unsolved puzzle with a few pieces missing. I was definitely fragmented.

Let me try to explain. Humans are a rare synergy of body, mind, emotion, and spirit: the whole being greater than the sum of the parts. When one part of the self is missing or diseased, the being is unwell. Each of us is made up of body, mind, soul, and spirit. The body is the recreational vehicle that moves us along Mother Earth. The mind is the ruler, creating every experience. The mind is heavily influenced by the ego, which is often inflated or deflated. The soul is an undiluted droplet of God living within us. The soul is perfect and unaffected by what the mind and body does. The spirit is our true self, the animating force within us. Secondhand alcoholism has great potential to harm the spirit. This is where I felt the most fragmented, some parts of me actually felt vacant, or at least damaged.

The word "disintegrated" came to mind. The dictionary describes "integrate" as "to make into a whole by bringing all parts together, to unify." I recalled reading books about how parts of the spirit or self will leave the body, especially after the person has experienced trauma or long-term abuse. In certain tribal societies, the shaman, who is a medium between the visible and the spirit worlds, "calls back the spirit" and the person becomes whole and well. I needed a shaman. But I also needed to name what was missing.

Women are so astonishing when they're fully intact. They are the closest humans will ever come to seeing, touching, and knowing the Great Goddess Herself. Women commonly find themselves strongly identifying with certain archetypes or standards, such as the Mother, the Lover, the Seductress, the High Priestess, the Warrior, the Wild Woman, the Crone, and the Teacher, to name a few. These archetypes are an integral part of a woman's identity. They help her to define herself, and to find her place in this world. Unfortunately, these archetypal energies can get ignored, chased away, or killed off. I identify with the Lioness archetype.

Do you strongly identify with one or more of these archetypes?

This is what author, Clarissa Pinkola Estes, has to say about such archetypes in her incredible book, *Women Who Run With the Wolves*: "We are all filled with a longing for the wild. There are few culturally sanctioned antidotes for this yearning. We were taught to feel shame for such a desire. We grew our hair long and used it to hide our feelings. But the shadow of Wild Woman still lurks behind us during out days and in our nights. No matter where we are, the shadow that trots behind us is definitely four-footed."

I think of these archetypes as spiritual energies or powers bestowed upon us by God, or instilled in us by our ancestors. These powers can be unsettling, especially if the woman is attempting to play a role that she was not born to perform. For example, a career-minded woman marries a man who secretly wants her to be a stay-at-home wife. He may not even be consciously aware that he desires to tame and domesticate this somewhat wild woman that he fell in love with.

Although compromise is a necessity if you desire peaceful relationships, too much compromise creates insanity. If the wild woman is tamed against her true will, she will go mad like a caged animal. Alcoholism shoves otherwise healthy women into bottles, roles, and corsets that don't suit them. The result is tragic. What other things cause women not to be fully themselves? Anything and anyone they allow to.

Who and what we are is important to acknowledge. To be what we are is the key to happiness, in my humble opinion. Not knowing who you are can be as dangerous as not knowing where you're going. If you don't know whom you are or what you are here on earth to do, for God's sake, find out.

I suggest that you first get away from the maddening crowd. Go somewhere alone. Pray for answers. Mediate all day or all year, if needed. Open yourself up so that Divine Truth can enter your consciousness. If you ask, answers will come. But please try to refrain from judging the answers you are given. Remember, you are not smarter than God is, trust me on this one. Now with answers in hand, go home, and become fully yourself, no matter what.

For as long as I can remember, I have considered myself a "cat person." We have almost always had a kitten or a cat in the house. However, my love affair with felines extends way beyond the realm of the house cat into the wild lands where the wild cats roam. So naturally, I tend to closely identify with the Lioness archetype.

I don't remember a time in my life when I didn't know that I was a lioness at heart. I once walked this earth like a lioness traversing her private savanna. I felt invincible, and I was. I knew how to hunt, defend my territory, nurture my young, and live in harmony with my surroundings. I didn't back away from danger (fear), but rather I rushed towards it and conquered it. I roared like thunder.

Now when I looked into a mirror, I saw a puddy-tat, not a lioness. I meowed. When I peered into my own soul, I saw my Lioness Within lying on her back, all four paws outstretched, deeply asleep. She no longer purred in contentment. She slept and dreamed of victorious hunts from days gone by, of birthing her cubs, of playing in the tall grass with her sister lionesses, and fiercely mating with new lions. She was trapped in a cool, grassy dream world, disconnected from the present and her true nature.

There is much myth, folklore, and fairy tales about lions. Many kings and queens throughout history have used the lion as a symbol of strength and courage. The lion is the only animal that relies extensively on group cooperation. The family group is referred to as the *pride*. Lionesses tend to stay in the pride that they were born in, which creates a group consisting of sisters, aunts, cousins, mothers, and grandmothers.

These females display a sense of devotion to each other, and commonly care for each other's cubs. The members of the pride live, play, hunt, and deal with hardships together. The female cubs stay in the pride, while the male cubs are forced out to prevent incest, and to breed with the females from other prides. This ensures the survival of this species.

The role of the lion is quite different than that of the lioness. He mates with the pride's females (his wives), guards the territory against strange lions attempting to enter their hunting ground, plays with the cubs, and eats the meat provided by the lionesses. Sick or weak males are driven out of the pride. (TJ is lucky not to have been born a lion in this lifetime.)

There is an interesting story about the male lion's behavior. An old, frail lion will pose on one end of the jungle, and let out the fierce roars. The trembling creatures within the jungle (his would-be prey) will hear the roars, and run swiftly to the other end of the terrain, desperately attempting to escape from sure death. On the far end of the jungle await the young, strong lions ready to capture an easy meal. Unsuspecting prey, running from the old lion's roar, fall unexpectedly into the hungry jaws of the younger lions. The moral of the story: Never run from your fears, it may be sending you into a dangerous situation.

Unfortunately, the lion has no job security. Every few years, the prime male lion leaves the pride, either by force or resignation, and a new prime male enters the picture. This changing of the guard, so to speak, is Mother Nature's way of improving the genetics of future cubs. Survival of the fittest, that's the name of their game.

The lioness image is that of the royal matriarch. Her common characteristics are beauty, strength, courage, confidence, grace, intuition, spiritedness, and loyalty to her family. These are characteristics that I highly value and seek to cultivate in myself.

Real lionesses in their natural habitat have so much to teach modern woman. They can help women understand how putting their own basic needs, before the needs of their children is a selfless not a selfish thing to do. I believe that too many women feel that they must sacrifice, suffer, and sometimes die for their children and mates, which they do, of course, in the name of love.

I was horrified to discover that being a stay-at-home-mom is the most risky job you can have. It's even riskier than being a taxi driver or a convenience store clerk. The stay-at-home-mom's life span is shorter than women who choose other professions. What makes this profession so risky? Job dissatisfaction. In other words, not being who you are, not liking who you are, or not being appreciated or respected. Don't get me wrong, some great and happy mothers still exist, but not as many as this planet needs. Perhaps the ones who do stay at home, like I did, must find a way to stay strong and fully intact.

In her book, *The Lion Family Book*, Angelika Hofer writes, "The lionesses have killed a gnu and eaten most of it themselves, but now it is the cubs' turn. Only when the lionesses have had enough meat will there be something left over for the young lions. So even a mother lion thinks of herself first. It seems selfish, but think about it: How can the pride survive unless the hunters and defenders of the area are strong and well-fed?"

Excellent question. How can our family units survive if the matriarchs are weak or unhealthy?

The Lioness Within motivates women to fiercely protect the people and things that she loves. It instills in her a killer instinct, although she will deny it to the end. If she has to, she will hunt and even kill to protect her territory, her young, and her feeble relatives. She will prowl the land, seeking cool grasses and an abundant supply of food and water. She seeks a mate when the season is right, but never allows the mate to change her focus or her perception of who she is.

She lives by her wits and the wisdom passed down to her by her ancestors. She is magnificent, strong, beautiful, dangerous when necessary, and brave, the queen of her chosen jungle. Her cubs adore her. Her enemies respect her. The Universe gladly fulfills her wishes.

Some examples of a modern-day women who I believe live (or lived) a leonine life style are: Oprah Winfrey, Linda McCartney, Susan B. Anthony, Her Royal Highness Princess Diana, Mother Teresa, Jacqueline Kennedy, Shirley MacClaine, Hillary Rodham Clinton, and Elisabeth Kulber-Ross.

So how do you wake a sleeping Lioness Within?

You call out her name. My children and friends tried to wake me up to what was happening to me. They saw the affect that secondhand alcoholism was having on my spirit, and called out to me, but I pretended to be deaf.

You shake her awake. My failing health and bouts with depression shook me up, but I refused to connect these illnesses with their true causes. It was easier to be physically ill than mentally and spiritually well. Nap time.

You startle her awake. TJ's arrests startled me awake, enraged and engaged me for a while, but then I'd dozed back off. Why watch if the movie stinks?

You harm her or her pride (family). Through the drinking years, I tried to buffer my children from the effects of their stepfather's alcoholism. I chose instead to take the brunt of the beating myself. Until now, I don't believe that my children or my parents ever really knew the true nature of my situation. However, if the harm was done directly to them, instead of to me, I think I would have rose up sooner to reclaim our peace and sanity. This is probably the topic of a separate book, but I must also mention that my children did suffer the effects of third-hand alcoholism.

You call upon God and the angels for assistance. Many times I cried out to God and to the angels for help. I begged for TJ to be healed. However, by Christmas 1999, I was begging for my own healing, too. That's when the celestial troops rushed in with a miracle or two.

Is your Lion or Lioness Within awake?

To get my Lioness energy re-booted, I implemented an A.A. slogan into my thinking: "Fake it 'til you make it." So I pretended at first that a magnificent lioness lived within in me. I decided to grow my hair out like a wild mane, wear animal prints, carry myself with the grace and dignity of a lion queen, act a little wild, and when I was alone, let out a mighty roar.

Becoming reconnected with my Lioness Within was a conscious choice that I made. I wanted her back with a passion. I invited her back with love. I needed her back, and told her so during meditation. And so she came back, creeping in during the night, slipping beneath the sheets of my fears, and merging with my spirit. A few days later, I wasn't too surprised to receive a call from the editor of Cat Fancy magazine who wanted to buy an article from me. I am woman! Hear me roar! When April ended, I had gained a new confidence.

11
JUST WHEN YOU THOUGHT IT WAS OVER

May 2000

HANDLING RELAPSE

May strut into this party like a vixen, looking to create a heap of trouble.

By then, TJ's beloved Harley-Davidson 2000 Sportster motorcycle had arrived. It was purple, loud, powerful, and he was in Harley Heaven. He named it "Dino." In his mind, this bike was symbolic of his recovery. It represented freedom, strength, and new life. To T.J, the Harley-Davidson wing symbol was as important to him as the recovery symbol--the triangle inside the circle. He even contemplated joining a biker's A.A. group, which existed in the Twin Cities.

TJ had proven that he was an alchemist, transforming his humble self into something royal. Instead of always assuming the role of the lead bird, splitting the wind in two for others to follow, I took a back seat--literally. I rode behind him on the bike, and it was a very sensual experience, no doubt.

This bike roared like a lioness in heat, the seat vibrated beneath our butts, my inner knees cradled his behind, and my breasts pressed against his back as our bodies melded into one another. While we road, Mother Nature flaunted her beauty, curves, valleys, and secret spots like a woman in love.

The world looks different when you are on a motorcycle. I didn't know how much I was missing when I was in a car--the wind, luscious greenery, hyperactive birds, sunrises and sunsets, magnificent cloud formations, butterflies and wild flowers of every color, and the faces of real people peering out at us through their car windows. We casually exchange nods and peace symbols.

I felt so much more too, the heat, the chill, the humidity, the bumps and curves in the road. My senses were tickled. Sometimes, everything I saw looked fantastic, as if I was viewing a piece of art. Riding aroused me from my everyday slumber. I was waking up.

Riding together was also a spiritual experience for us. TJ used to say, "I bet Jesus would ride a Harley if he were born in this time." He compared motorcycle riders to the rebels that followed Jesus. They both took a different road than the masses, they didn't quite fit the stereotype of a traditional man, and their hearts thumped with passion and purpose.

Sometimes, I'd hear TJ shouting with joy as we rode. "Yeee-haaa!" he'd yell, proclaiming his liberation to an indifferent world. It was exhilarating fun to see him filled with such uninhibited elation. Moreover, I was surprised to find my life-long fear of motorcycles was utterly absent. Even though I knew the dangers of riding, I felt no fear, none whatsoever. I believed that our angels road beside us, undoubtedly relieved that our lives were getting interesting again.

Then on May 1st Lord Alcohol abruptly reappeared in my life, and sucker-punched me. I doubled over in pain when I learned that he had just killed my former co-worker and friend. Leanne was only forty years old and had sparkled like golden amber in the sunlight. She appeared to have it all—looks, personality, a great mate, money, success, and a big family.

She also had alcoholism, like an ancient bug trapped in this golden gem of a person. On three separate occasions, she tried rehab without much success. For the past year she had maintained her sobriety. Then three weeks before her death, she slipped big time and couldn't get back up. The coroner called it suicide, but I called it murder.

Leanne's death reminded me how much I truly hate this disease. (As if I could forget!) I swear, if the cruelty of alcoholism were widely known, the entire human population would rise up and find a goddamn cure for it. My feelings about Leanne's death were eclectic. I felt compassion for her loved ones; love for her; hostility towards her disease; and a sad sense of relief that her suffering had ended. No one suffers quite like an addict. Without a doubt, she put up an awesome fight against a heartless, fire-breathing opponent, and I was proud of her. Who really knows who won and who lost this war?

On May 5th, we took a thirty-five mile ride on the Harley to West St. Paul to attend the traditional Cinco de Mayo festival. Cinco de Mayo is the Mexican holiday comparable to our Independence Day. TJ was born and raised in West St. Paul, but moved to an upscale suburb when he was twelve.

What surprised me this year was that TJ *wanted* to attend the celebration, as if he had suddenly acquired an interest in his heritage. Up until May 5, 2000, TJ viewed Cinco de Mayo as a day to legitimately guzzle margaritas all night long, not as a day to celebrate your nationality.

I watched him sampling his rich cultural heritage of Mexico, as if tasting some new, spicy recipe. First a look, then a wee taste, then a big bite...and he liked it! As a child, he said that he grew up ashamed to be Mexican in a predominantly white world. But now he was obviously pleased to be a Mexican-American. In innocent awe, I wandered with him amid a sea of brown-skinned people. I couldn't help but wonder if I looked like a speck of lint on a black velvet garment.

We met his various relatives around nearly every corner. He appeared to be somehow related to everyone. Lively Tex-Mex and traditional Mexican music could be heard on every corner. Pretty raven-haired senoritas flirted with their dark-eyed Don Juans or fussed over their babies. The food was hot, greasy, and aromatic, while the Coronas were highly visible and abundant. Untreated alcoholism ran rampant in this Hispanic community, I have heard. Silently, I pondered the fate of TJ' s many nephews and nieces.

Tattoos decorated many bare arms and backs, boasting the bearer's devotion to Mother Mary, to a gang, or to his or her pedigree. The heated air was cooled by the swish of the long, colorful skirts worn by the dancers. I felt as if I had stepped off the edge of reality and onto a movie set.

So there I was, hand in hand, with my swarthy husband. I was his physical opposite: blonde, pale-skinned, and green-eyed with a touchy stomach. I didn't know Spanish. I couldn't eat the food. I didn't look like the people. All in all, I felt like an alien in this Little Mexico.

"I feel sort of out of place here," I eventually admitted to TJ

"If anyone asks, just tell him or her that your name is Martinez," he offered with a sly grin.

"No one would believe me."

A week later, I was faced with another dilemma: I had to decide if I should file a law suit for negligence against the state-ran housing program that neglected to check on my dad, which resulted in him lying dead on his bedroom floor for 24 to 30 hours before we found him. I'm not sue-happy, quite the contrary. But the situation haunted me.

His sudden death was difficult enough to accept without the added pain of knowing he laid there undiscovered for so long, like a homeless person in a lonesome alley. Murder victims are found sooner than he was. Stray dogs at the Humane Society are checked on more often than he was. Finally, I asked myself: What would dad do if this had happened to my mother or to one of his kids? The answer didn't slowly come to me, but rather it exploded inside my head: "Do it!" So I did.

Then on May 19th, TJ relapsed. (Jesus, I hate that sentence!) The previous evening, a wickedly full moon had debuted overhead, impregnating susceptible minds with lunar madness. TJ was an easy target--sick, tired, and home alone. He had had a touch of the flu, and decided to take the day off work to get better.

He admitted to me that I after I had left for work that he had made the insane decision to drink. So he drove up to the liquor store, bought a bottle of rum, mixed it with a 2-liter bottle of Fresca, and stored it in our refrigerator. What he hadn't counted on was my getting home early from work, and my ability to spot a drunk a mile away. Well, he was busted all right, but was already too drunk to deal with.

I'll never forget how he looked, or how I felt seeing him lying in our bed, repulsively drunk. To say I was merely shocked, enraged, or hurt would be like calling a murder/suicide a lover's spat. I was livid as I ceremoniously dumped his moonshine down the kitchen drain, hid the car and motorcycle keys, made a bed for myself on the living room couch, and then prayed like an innocent woman on death row.

That night, I slept about two hours at the most. The rest of the night was spent questioning myself, questioning TJ's sanity and motives, questioning God, and eventually telling God to shove "a Power greater than ourselves could restore us to sanity" business up his holy ass. That night I had one dream: I dreamt that my throat was slit.

Morning erupted like a nuclear bomb in our bedroom. I was shell-shocked and ready to fight. The Lioness Within had her teeth showing and her claws sharpened. I was high on adrenaline and rage. He was hung-over and defensive.

The first hour consisted of hissing, growling, pouncing, and going for the throat, followed by a brutal verbal beating, a Gestapo-like interrogation, a forced confession, and banishment from the pride. I never knew how truly clever I was at verbally lacerating someone. Later, I apologized for saying such deplorable things to him...even if they were the goddamn truth.

Meanwhile, TJ had a giant hangover. Apparently, the Antabuse that he had been taking for the past five months kicked in, and made him violently ill. Body fluids were gushing out of every spout. And I was secretly pleased to see him suffer. This went on for hours and hours. {Antabuse is a drug used to treat alcoholics. It causes uncomfortable symptoms, including flushing, headache, nausea, and vomiting if a person drinks alcohol while taking the drug. In some instances, the patient has to be hospitalized.)

After all the retching and moaning stopped, I asked TJ why he had decided to drink. He said he didn't know why. What a jackass, I thought. He betrays everyone and everything dear to him in the world, especially him self, and doesn't even know why. What an idiot. What a typical alcoholic.

The rest of the day was morbidly melodramatic. I felt hopeless. I entertained suicidal and murderous thoughts. I asked him for a divorce. I fought him like he was my mortal enemy instead of immortal lover. I prayed, "God, grant me the serenity not to kill him..." Apparently, nothing had changed after all. He was still getting loaded and I was still getting pissed off.

That afternoon TJ talked to his sponsor, and met him at an A.A. meeting later that evening. TJ said he never had a craving, but thought that perhaps the prospect of being home alone all day, triggered the relapse. Apparently, in his drinking days, when he stayed home "sick" from work, what he was really doing was drinking to unconsciousness. I didn't understand these so-called "triggers."

The following morning, we attended an open A.A. Speaker/Breakfast together. While there, I was reminded that alcoholism is characterized by episodes of relapse. Cancer patients often go into remission, and then relapse for no apparent reason. So do alcoholics. That's the nature of this beast.

When I am at an A.A. event I feel as if I have illegally entered a foreign country. I know I am and will always be an outsider, a "normie" or a bastard who can drink socially. I found that the people who do belong to this exclusive subculture are lively, upbeat, and seemingly proud of their affiliation. Some of the people there did cause me to wonder if they were addicted to A.A. But it was all good. After the meeting, TJ and his sponsor shot a round of golf. The calm after the storm was starting to settle over us.

In retrospect, I think this "slip" taught us both a great lesson. It was a lesson about power. TJ saw the awesome power of Step 1 in action. *We admitted we were powerless over alcohol--that our lives had become unmanageable.* Apparently, he had forgotten the "powerless over alcohol" part. After the motorcycle--his symbol of recovery--arrived, I noticed that he lost interest in his recovery.

Where A.A. once held him up, now the bike did. As a result, I think he became overconfident. The bike made him feel powerful, maybe even led him to think that he was now powerful enough to beat alcohol. So, he mistakenly tested his theory. But once again, Lord Alcohol slammed him to the mat, and stomped the living shit out of him.

This "slip" was a lesson in power for me, too. I was once again reminded that I, too, am powerless over TJ's alcoholism. It was like watching a movie. You watch it, you become involved in the story, but you can't affect the outcome. Moreover, I saw clearly my tendency, especially when I'm under duress, to tap into ego power instead of soul (God) power. The end result is always lackluster, to say the least.

In this particular incident, I thought my reaction to the "slip" was unenlightened. Sometimes, even for an old metaphysics veteran like myself, it's hard to distinguish the voice of ego from the voice of soul, as the ego is a great impersonator. But if you can calm down enough to really listen, a person can identify who is doing the internal talking. Here are some guideposts:

The ego is an aspect of the human mind. The soul is an aspect of the mind of God.

The ego is focused on the body--how it looks and feels, its comings and goings, and preventing its decay and demise. The soul focuses on the spirit (the real you) and the spirit's relationship with the Source Spirit.

The ego tends to be closed and negative. The soul is always open and positive.

The ego creates conflict and commotion. The soul creates peace.

The ego demands and nags. The soul encourages.

The ego is erratic. The soul is consistent.

The ego is critical. The soul is accepting.

The ego is tight and fearful. The soul is expansive and loving.

The ego fights. The soul compromises.

The ego controls. The soul sets you free.

The ego chatters endlessly and says nothing of consequence. The soul whispers chosen words of God.

The ego demands respect. The soul respects you.

The ego is opposed to your enlightenment. The soul applauds enlightenment.

The ego desires power. The soul is your true source of power.

Once you've begun to listen to voice of your soul, and start taking its advice, you will begin to feel lighter, clearer, better.

A few days later, a drunk driver in a head-on collision a few miles from my home killed Malik Sealy, a player from the Minnesota Timberwolves basketball team. When will it ever end? When will alcoholism be a curable disease? And who will stop the alcoholic's insane behavior if people are afraid of appearing co-dependent if they try a little too hard? In my son Jake's words, "That's whacked!" Go in peace, Malik. Your life mattered to all of us. So did your death.

How bizarre was this? On May 24th, I was sitting on the floor of my living room, packing a box for storage. My female cat, Sedona, was sitting beside me, looking on. Suddenly, an electronic gadget inside the box started to chatter. Shocked by the loud voice inside a seemingly innocent box, Sedona jumped straight up in the air, landed on my lap, leapt off, using my left hip as a springboard, then ran out of the room. It all happened in a second, but when that second ended, I knew I had been injured in the fiasco.

White, hot pain sprang from my hip. When I looked down at the source, I saw four bleeding puncture wounds from Sedona's back claws. A bit stunned and bleeding, I rushed to clean and bandage the wounds. All day my hip throbbed with pain. By dinnertime, I removed the bandages and discovered that the wound was purple, hot, and the size of a baseball.

A very concerned TJ drove me to a nearby Urgent Care Center. When the nurse saw my wound, she blurted out, "Oh, my God!" When the physician saw my wound, he blurted out, "Oh, my God!" When your doctor makes a statement like that, you know you're in trouble. Apparently, Sedona's claws had punctured a vein or maybe even an artery.

Luckily, the internal bleeding had stopped, but now I was at risk for blood poisoning, bacterial infection, and a host of other gruesome maladies. I felt queasy when I read the doctor's nametag. His name was Dr. Rabie. Comforting. After getting a tetanus shot and antibiotics to ward off infection, I headed home, feeling as if I had been attacked by a Siberian Tiger, instead of a six-pound house cat.

Believing that each illness and accident is a reflection of what's happening in your mind and life, I decided that TJ's relapse a few days before had left me feeling as if I had been kicked in the ass. The now softball-size bruise on my hip did mirror my feelings: sore, hot, throbbing, bruised, and unsightly.

12
HOW SWEET THE MADNESS

June 2000

SLIPPING WITHOUT HITTING ROCK BOTTOM

A strange and sweet madness came over me in June. The true source of the madness eluded me at the time. Was it PMS, grief, TJ's relapse, the moon, or the cat attack? Maybe it was all of the above. I wondered if people could tell how hysterical and crazy I truly was inside. I felt unquestionably crackers. Perhaps sanity is overrated after all.

For example, I had been thinking about getting a tattoo on my butt. The image would be a black "X" with the words "Kiss Here" written in elegant, looping lettering. Am I mad? I even thought of a tattoo for TJ's: simply the word "Dog." I must've been real mad at him. No matter.

I also became obsessed with seeing the face of God. I felt like the Sufi poet, Rumi, who yearned to meet God in human form. Later, such a supreme human being did appear in Rumi's life in the form of the powerful, wandering dervish, Shams of Tabriz. But that was 1244 and this is 2000. Where on earth does one find Shams today? In an Internet chat room, at Starbucks sipping coffee, at the mall, or in the produce section at Cub.

I know that there are beloved people alive today, such as Sai Baba, His Holiness the Dalai Lama, and Thich Nhat Hahn, but where is *my* Shams? Where is my miracle worker? I just wanted to know so that I could stop peering into the eyes of not-so-perfect strangers, looking, longing, and wondering if.

Have you ever seen the movie "The Truman Show" starring Jim Carrey? He plays a character named Truman Banks who was born on a gargantuan movie set, and spent his first thirty years unaware that he wasn't living in a real world. The show's creator, Chrystos, orchestrated Truman's life in a god-like manner, while gathering high ratings and personal power.

I sometimes wonder if we're all a little like Truman Banks, acting in our little play we call life, while an omnipotent God looks on, adjusting the weather when need be, killing off unnecessary characters, and tossing in drama and trauma during ratings week. Sometimes He helps out. Sometimes He doesn't do a damn thing. Apparently, He is quite moody. Perhaps this is all an illusion like the great prophets have said. Is any of it real? Am I real? Is God? Just asking...

There was no logical reason for my obsession to see the face of God, unless I had come down with a rapidly growing case of spiritual madness. I looked up the word "madness" in my American Heritage dictionary, and found a number of meanings for this word. Most of the meanings described me quite nicely. They were: 1. Angry, resentful. 2. Suffering from a disorder of the mind; insane. 3. Temporarily or apparently deranged by violent sensations, emotions, or ideas. 4. Lacking restraint or reason; foolish. 5. Feeling or showing strong liking or enthusiasm. 6. Marked by extreme excitement, confusion, or agitation; frantic. 7. Crazy.

Yes, I was angry, resentful, foolish, and crazy. But mostly I was angry. My anger was like a tapeworm devouring my insides. It was fiery and blinding. I thought that I was done being angry, but apparently I was not. I even resented my anger. I couldn't help but wonder to what degree my warring thoughts were polluting the atmosphere. All I could do, short of harming myself or someone else, was to walk it off.

So I walked and cried and initiated a conversation with God. "Hello, up there. It's me again." I walked with angels and they held my hands. "There, there, sweet girl," they whispered in my ears. I shouted at God about my rage. "I am so mad I could throw myself into a burning bush!" I walked with demons and they laughed at me and tightened their grip on my mind. "My, our girl is feisty."

Jesus' cries began to sound strangely like my own, "My God, my God, why hast thou forsaken me?" (Mark 15:30 KJV) I begged God to send my Rumi, to send my Shams. I walked with Mother Nature, my only earthly mother, and She called me her child. Oh, how I longed for my childhood. God, how I missed my parents! I asked God to reinvent me. He said, "Again?" And I was embarrassed. When my walk was over, I was once again room temperature.

Anger is a lethal emotion. I can now see that I had created some nasty karma with my anger and unwillingness to be happy. Just a week and a half after the infamous cat attack, I was once again at the Urgent Care Center with a six-inch gash in my lower leg. The attending physician asked me if I had an accident with a lawn mower. (Since I don't believe in accidents, but rather believe that we create all aspects of our life, I use the word accident quite loosely.)

This is how this sad story goes: I opened a kitchen cupboard door and a glass vase rolled out and shattered on the floor. I carefully picked up the pieces and put them in a bag. However, when I picked up the bag to bring it to the trash can, the glass ripped through the bag, and then through my leg, cutting me to the bone. The ironic part was that the vase was actually a wine carafe that I used as a vase. Lord Alcohol must surely have been playing some kind of Cosmic joke on me.

I panicked at the sight of so much blood spurting out the gaping wound. I was home alone at the time, but managed to call TJ at work, which was forty-five minutes away from our home. "I'm in big trouble!" I blurted out to him, but he was too far away to help me. So pumped with fear and adrenaline, I sat on the floor, bound up the gash as best I could, and then drove myself to the Urgent Care Center. The cut was deep and ragged, and it took many stitches to close the wound.

As you might imagine, this second freaky mishap in ten days forced me to search for the cause of my bad karma. It took me barely thirty seconds to realize that since TJ's relapse, I had been very angry with him. Like a firebrand, I fought with him every day for two weeks, inciting riots and causing commotion, most likely in an unconscious attempt to punish him for upsetting my proverbial apple cart. He had gotten so weary and punch-drunk by my violence that he even suggested that we separate. That, I must admit, was another Kodak rock-bottom moment, for sure.

Rumi's words again rumbled through mind, "Don't try to put out a fire by throwing on more fire!" It's true. I had been throwing anger on my anger, and wondering why my life was so tumultuous. I had been approaching my husband with closed fists, instead of open arms.

On the drive home from Urgent Care, I started listening to the audio book, *The Art of Happiness*, by His Holiness the Dalai Lama. From the hollows of my dashboard, he urged me to release my anger and I relented. A moment later, I suddenly began to have the weirdest sensation that the anger that had coursed through my bloodstream for weeks was now exiting with the blood that seeped from my wound. I bled long after the wound was sutured, and when the bleeding finally stopped, I felt more alive and saner than I had in weeks. Perhaps this bloodletting, albeit unintentional, turned out to be emotionally therapeutic.

That evening, TJ and I attended a wedding. The groom and bride, who were acquaintances of TJ's, were both in their mid-twenties. Although it was a rather small wedding, what was so startling to me was the number of addicts in attendance, starting with the bride. She was about one hundred pounds over-weight. Even beneath her extravagant bridal gown, it was impossible to hide her food addiction. That would be like trying to hide a car under a silk scarf.

At various times during the evening, I would see her with one cigarette in each hand, or a glass of champagne in each hand. The groom's drug of choice seemed to be beer, but unlike his bride, he only made a half-ass of himself. Fortunately for the newlyweds, excessive alcohol consumption causes next-day amnesia. They made me realize how little tolerance I have for drunks.

About ninety percent of the wedding guests appeared to be Nicotine Anonymous dropouts. Having never been a smoker, I wondered what this drug did for them, and why they sacrificed their lives for it. I saw chain-smokers who appeared to inhale the fumes right down to their toenails, as if they were sucking in oxygen after being underwater for three minutes.

I saw so much alcohol go down the hatch that I wondered how these party-people kept from wetting their pants. I witnessed outrageous behavior: mothers dancing sensuously with sons, husbands grabbing the asses of other men's wives, and children watching this mayhem unfold and learning, by example, how adults act at weddings.

I, of course, felt out of place there--being sober and all. Time and time again, someone would offer TJ and I alcoholic beverages, and then seem genuinely insulted when we politely declined their offers. "Come on, you guys, have a drink! It's a wedding!" Non-drinkers are a shrinking minority. Maybe we ought to form a union or start a revolution to bolster our cause. I think we ought to be respected or at least tolerated, not snubbed and criticized. No wonder it's so hard to stay sober in such an alcohol-soaked society.

It's not that I am against all addictions. We all have a few small ones--coffee, diet sodas, Hostess cupcakes, and shoes. A totally non-addicted human is a dead human. But rather I'm for freedom and moderation. What joy to be able to live happily with or without something or someone? This must be the kind of freedom that the Buddha often spoke about. He called it detachment, warm and loving detachment. I liked that idea.

On June 6th, we bought a condominium near TJ's new job. It was perfect for us. However, by June 11th, TJ had cold feet. He didn't want to buy the house, because that would mean he would be financially obligated to stay with me. Apparently, he had decided that he wanted a divorce. His recovery wasn't going well. It seemed as if the initial excitement had worn off, and he had started to feel real feelings, which, of course, he didn't like.

I tried to explain to him that everyone experiences every emotion, and that these feelings are normal. In other words, he's normal. But he didn't buy that explanation. He wanted a quicker fix; the kind that alcohol could provide. Now he saw me as standing in the way between him and the bottle. Suddenly, I was the problem, not the booze. He wanted me out, and Lord Alcohol back in.

He admitted that he has been using alcohol again since he saw a segment on 60 Minutes about how certain alcoholics can learn to be "wise drinkers." That idea thrilled him to the core, so he began testing the theory. One a day. Maybe two. Or three. What were the test results? He went to sleep drunk every night.

After five years without a driver's license, and after only two months with one, he was also back to drinking and driving. But this time he was not only driving a car, he was also driving a motorcycle under the influence. And I thought I was the insane one in our family.

Of course, I didn't take the drinking and divorce news well. If anyone in this family was going to do the drinking and divorcing, it was going to be me, not him. After all, I reasoned, I had stuck the marriage out for nearly seven drunken years, and I deserved to experience the sober times. Enlightened or not, that was how I was thinking.

I was, however, surprised that the anger that I had recently dissipated, didn't return. But the hurt did. TJ had asked me for a divorce ever since he married me, although he never acted on his supposed intention. I had come to understand that the booze was asking, not TJ. Still, this habit of solving difficulties by running or threatening to run has left me feeling unsafe in the relationship, even though he professed to love me.

Desperate for anything that might ease my pain, I drove an hour to Stillwater for a psychic reading. Diane, the psychic there, was round and ordinary in appearance. All the psychics that I had ever known were quite quirky. My initial impression was that she would not be able to help me. But I was wrong.

When she first tuned in to me psychically, she said she saw the image of me on a teeter-totter. The masculine aspect was big and forceful, dumping raw emotion in the face of the feminine aspect, which was head-down and bound with ropes to one end of the teeter-totter. She interpreted this symbol to indicate a major imbalance of masculine and feminine energies within me. The masculine represented logic, and the feminine represented intuition and emotion. Apparently, there was a war going on between a bully and a damsel in distress inside me.

I proceeded to explain the hard facts to her: I was married to an alcoholic. He went into recovery on January 1, but was currently out of recovery. I told her that I was on a quest for knowledge. I either needed to learn how to live peacefully and happily with my husband, or learn how to leave him. I also told her how sick he was and how he needed serious help.

Then she nodded and proceeded to tell me how sick *I* was and how *I* needed serious help. She didn't ask me about the alcoholism that ran rampant in TJ's family. She asked about the alcoholism in mine. I did my best to camouflage my offended feelings.

"Both of my grandfathers were alcoholics, but they've been dead for thirty-some years. My parent's weren't drinkers nor are any of their children, including me."

"So you were raised by two parents who were Adult Children of Alcoholics (ACoA)."

"Well, yes, technically," I sheepishly admitted, "but they were both quite normal and functional people."

"That may appear true, but they undoubtedly were affected by their parents' alcoholism, just like you are by your husbands, right?"

"I guess they were, but they didn't show it."

"They probably showed it in subtle ways--ways that you are not aware of yet. Perhaps they passed along to you some co-dependent ways of thinking and behaving."

I cringed. "I hate that label!"

She smiled. "Then find out why you hate it. Go see a counselor. Not a marriage counselor, but one who deals with chemical dependency."

"But I'm not chemically dependent!" I protested.

"Then go see a counselor."

Damn, she made me feel like squirrel trapped on the center island between two lanes of highway. Both lanes were packed with people in cars, speeding like mad, completely unaware that I existed. Perhaps I have become invisible after all. What's a squirrel to do?

I weighed my options. I could stand there frozen with fear on the center island (paralyzed). I could pretend that I was elsewhere (delusional). I could dash across the road, and hope to make it alive to the side of the road (reckless). I could throw myself into oncoming traffic (suicide).

I could shake my tail just so, hitch a ride, and go somewhere with someone (adultery). I could act like a maniac, until the police arrived to arrest me (passive aggressive). I could throw shoes and stones at the passing cars (aggressive). I could dig a hole and hide in it (denial). I could call out for help (smart action). Or I could raise my hands and face towards the sky and surrender (wise action).

"Okay, I'll go," I acquiesced.

On June 11, 2000, I surrendered. I accepted that I may be powerless over my husband's alcohol addiction, but I was not powerless over my own attachments and delusions. Suddenly, I had crystal clear awareness of the nature of my own suffering. I created or allowed it to be, and I could un-create and un-allow it. I was through with my Saint Joan of Arc syndrome. Getting burned alive at the stake had suddenly lost its appeal.

On June 12th, I set up an appointment with a counselor, who facilitated co-dependency groups. The appointment was set for six weeks away. That day I also attended my first Al-Anon meeting in three years. I felt quite out of place at the meeting. The topic of discussion was anger. The speaker told her story about being the child of an alcoholic. She said she never felt anger and couldn't express it. Part of her recovery was to learn how to feel and express anger. I was dumbfounded. How could someone not feel or express an emotion? My problem, as I saw it, was feeling and expressing too much emotion.

I left the meeting feeling ambivalent. I didn't want to go back and I didn't way to stay away. Compared to the A.A. meetings that I had attended with TJ, this Al-Anon meeting was quite subdued...even boring. At the A.A. meetings there was an almost party-like atmosphere; Al-Anon was serious and party-less. I guess the drunks were still having most of the fun, even when they're sober.

Although I wasn't jazzed about my first Al-Anon meeting, the literature that they sent home with me lit an ember of hope in me. I quickly read everything in the "Welcome Newcomer!" Packet. I was especially drawn to the pamphlet, "So You Love An Alcoholic" by Al-Anon Family Groups. It was all quite benign until I came to the section, "Some Important 'Don'ts.'" It suggested things like don't treat the alcoholic like a child; don't check up to see how much he is drinking; don't search for hidden liquor; don't pour liquor away; don't nag the alcoholic about the drinking; don't argue while he or she is drunk, etc.

It took a great deal of humility for me to admit to myself, and to TJ, that I had mastered every "Don't" on this list. I talked with him about the list, and about how my failure to seek real help, thus far, may have hindered his recovery. We both agreed that it was a good thing for me to be seeking professional help. I also liked the daily readings in the two Al-Anon books, *One Day At A Time In Al-Anon* and *Courage to Change*.

I spent my first Father's Day without my father. First motherless. Now I was fatherless, too. Who said less is more? I think it was Lao-tzu. Anyway, I wanted more.

Recently, the book, *Midlife Orphan* by Jane Brooks, had made its way into my hands. I skimmed the first few pages, steeling myself against the emotions that I feared the book would arouse. I didn't want to feel the pain of bereavement. I just wanted to intellectually understand it.

The author wrote, "We are indeed orphaned when our last parent dies and it takes time to adjust to our altered status from adult child to adult. In this new role, we are forced to step up to the helm, where we can no longer deny death--or its antithesis, life and personal growth--that is the legacy of this rite of passage. Our only choice is to seize our legacy."

Seize our legacy. Those words tantalized the befuddled Lioness Within. I paused to ask myself, what legacy did my parents leave to me? The answers came easily: They handed down to me their optimism, their fighting spirit, their humor, their generosity, their love of family and God, and their shining example of how a married couple can live together joyously for fifty-plus years. They were holy and outrageous and genuine and I was so blessed to be their girl. Happy Father's Day. Happy Daughter's Day.

Unfortunately, TJ's compulsion to drink had begun to dominate our lives once again. He was back to drinking every day, and back to blacking out every night. No matter how much he drank--one, two, or three--he would pass out for five or six hours, and be then sick. Gone were the days of a dozen beers at the club or on the golf course. I knew that his disease had progressed into a stage that I couldn't bear to accept.

Afraid and desperate, I swallowed my wounded pride and called another one of TJ's relatives to ask for help. A few days later, TJ's dad confronted his son, and asked him to go into treatment. TJ agreed to go, but not before one last binge. He arrived at home sloshed and passed out. I went to sleep that night utterly fed up. Not even Al-Anton's grandiose slogans could alleviate the pain of watching my beloved slowly kill himself before my eyes. That evening, there was no serenity in my home or in my heart. Only suffering.

That night, I had this dream: TJ and I were out together and we ran into his mother and other family members. His mother asked TJ to go drinking with the group. I said, "Honey, don't go," but he went anyway. I watched, disgusted, as the merry group left the building and walked outside. When they were about a block away, I saw a flock of hostile birds attack the family. It looked like the re-creation of the old Alfred Hitchcock movie, "The Birds." Then I turned to this stranger nearby and excitedly said, "Wild birds have just attacked my in-laws!" I awoke from this dream, wondering if this was a premonition.

The next morning, TJ aroused from his stupor. He was a hurting human when he said to me, "I'm done drinking now. I know I'm very sick. I'm ready to do whatever you think I should do to get well." Although it was only 6:00am, I called for help. Two hours later, he was scheduled to enter inpatient chemical dependency treatment at a Minneapolis rehabilitation center for the next three weeks.

13
REHAB IS FOR QUITTERS

July 2000

GETTING HELP FROM PROFESSIONALS

Day 1. At 9:00am on June 27th, TJ and I entered the Fairview Riverside Recovery Center in Minneapolis, and he admitted himself as an inpatient. After we both answered a slew of questions, a nurse escorted us to his room. The room was white and stark. A narrow bed was the only piece of furniture. I thought it looked more like a jail cell, than a hospital room.

TJ turned to me and asked, "Are you sure I can't go to Hazelden?" He liked its country club-like setting and gourmet cuisine. I told him that this was the only facility that our medical insurance covered, and he nodded, quietly accepting his fate. "This wasn't suppose to be a vacation," he reminded himself out loud. He was told that he would spend three days in detox.

After a few minutes, I was politely ordered to leave. The brochure I was handed explained that I could visit my husband on Sundays between 2:00-5:00pm. This was Tuesday. The only other nights we had spent apart was when he was in jail, or away at a golf outing with his high school buddies. I left the center, shaken and weeping. I wondered for a nanosecond if I had done the right thing when he asked me to get him some help. In the next heartbeat, I knew that I had. The A.A. slogan "One Day At A Time" would take on great personal meaning as I darkly envisioned the next 21 days of lonely nights, worrisome days, and personal excavation.

Our home was so quiet; not even a meow was heard from either cat. TJ's big screen ever-on television was silent. The kitchen was quiet. No talking, no laughing, no teasing, no making love, no movie watching, no snacking, not even one telemarketer called. My home was finally a serene place...and I hated it.

Day 2. TJ was released from detox early. Apparently, he had already begun the detoxification process at home the day before he arrived at the center. He had had an entirely miserable day, the combination of a hangover, withdrawal symptoms, and brutal reality. All night long he had major sweats and chills. His intake nurse told him that he could've had seizures. But now on Day 2, he felt good. He was cheerful, optimistic, and easily adapting to the situation. We were both highly relieved when all his medical tests came back normal. I, for one, was certain that his liver was diseased by now. But it wasn't. My husband was one lucky dude!

I kept busy. I worked and walked and prayed and slept and chatted with TJ on the telephone. I often found myself teetering on the edge of despair when I thought about 19 more days without him. I wobbled, but I never fell down. I watched our favorite show, Survivors by myself and imagined that I, too, was a survivor, of sorts. I was marooned on planet earth with all its other suffering aliens, who are trying to find their way back to the Mother Ship. How silly and superficial we must appear from God's perspective. We must look like manic ants. I've heard that when ants lose the scent of their queen, they become confused and die. Maybe that's what happens to addicts: they lose the scent of their Queen (Goddess).

Day 3. I received a call that morning from a woman named Nancy, who told me that she was to be my new counselor. She had a cancellation that day, and invited me to take the appointment. I marveled at the exquisite timing, as my actual appointment was still four weeks away. Serendipitous.

Nancy turned out to be a sweet and salty woman. She was a recovered alcoholic and a self-described recovered "skid row co-dependent." She was also very open-minded. When I told her I came to counseling at the advice of a psychic, she was not shocked, nor condescending. She commented on how fortunate we both were that this psychic had been able to pin point the problem so easily, where in traditional therapy it might have taken months.

Nancy also thought that my current dilemmas and challenges were most likely from being the granddaughter of alcoholics, and of course, from being in an intimate relationship with an active alcoholic. During the gut-spilling hour, I held back the tears quite nicely until Nancy asked me, "Would you spend the rest of your life with your husband if he turned out to be a chronic relapser? When you see or hear about some derelicts, they're what we call chronic relapsers." I lost it. I hadn't consciously considered that possibility, because it seemed too impossible to consider.

"I couldn't take it!" I blubbered out.

"Would you stay with him if I could teach you how to take it, and how to detach with love?" The word "detach" plucked a pretty chord on my heartstrings.

"I follow Buddhist teachings, and the Buddha spoke often about the need for detachment." I paused to clarify my thinking. "Yes. I would stay with him the rest of my life if I could learn to detach from his alcoholism," I announced to myself and to my new counselor.

She smiled at me and said, "Let's begin." At that moment, I saw a little blue "angel light" over Nancy's right shoulder. My spirit friends sometimes pierce the veil between the physical and spirit worlds by showing me a flicker of blue light to make their presence known. Sometimes, especially during a crisis, blue angel lights sparkle and flit about in my room like celestial fireflies. So there Nancy was with an angel light on her shoulder. That was certainly a good omen.

I left the clinic after making second appointment, and registering for a six-week group for children of alcoholics and co-dependents. I was also told to read the book, *Grandchildren of Alcoholics*. I felt lighter when I left...and hopeful.

Day 4. I thought a lot about my grandfathers' alcoholism and how it was still impacting their decedents more than three decades after their deaths. I also thought about TJ's decision not to have biological children, in part, because of his inherited disease. For the first time, I understood his decision, and it made perfect and wise sense to me. Why intentionally pass on this horrific disease?

In the afternoon, I sneaked onto the grounds of the treatment center, and slipped away for twenty minutes with my husband. We just couldn't wait two more days until the designated family visiting time to see each other. This time together was golden. He was so calm and loving. Bad Andy had apparently left the building. (Bad Andy was the name we had given to the personality that came out when TJ drank. TJ thought of Bad Andy as his alter ego or his dark twin.)

We were like star-crossed lovers, kept apart by circumstances or destiny. He talked about his treatment, and I about life on the outside. What I really wanted to do was drag my husband into the nearby woods, and make outrageous love with him. Good medicine.

Day 5. I awoke from this dream. An evil man was after TJ and I. He unrelentingly pursued us, even though he was weak, ragged, and injured; like the character Glenn Close played in Fatal Attraction. With all his remaining strength, this man tried to catch and kill us. We ran from him, and tried to fight back, but he wouldn't leave us alone. Frantic to be rid of this evil one, I came up with an idea. I suggested to TJ that instead of hating the man and fighting him, we should love him and extend kindness towards him. I believed that that was the only was he would leave us alone.

When I was fully awake, it came to me that this man was Lord Alcohol. The message of this dream was to embrace, and even love the one who caused us so much agony, because Lord Alcohol was one our greatest teacher. When we learned our lessons about love and freedom, he would gladly leave us.

I found that being separated from my mate was like being marooned on Discovery Island. There may be treasures buried here, but I was hesitant to open any treasure chests. Remember Pandora's box or Gerardo's safe? All the ills of the world or nothing but dirt could be inside.

In the evening, TJ's mother called. She was a nice, but often overwhelmed woman. She began the conversation by offering to attend Family Day activities at the treatment center, but she also added that she was too busy to attend. She admitted to me that her family had "a small problem with alcohol."

"Small!" my mind screamed, but I held in the words. Calmly, I said, "TJ has a big, serious problem with alcohol." To strengthen my point, I relayed that his medical doctor was surprised that TJ wasn't in the early stages of liver disease. When she began to minimize the seriousness, I realized that she thought that *I* was the problem, not the alcoholism.

I tried hard to make some nice small talk, then hung up the telephone. I felt exhausted. Thinking over the conversation, I realized that TJ's mother blamed me for the trouble, just as I had blamed them for not helping more. Today I made my first real discovery. If blame is to be placed, then it should be placed on the alcoholic, not on his or her loved ones.

For a few minutes, I sat beside our open bedroom window and let the moonlight bathe me. Then a question came to mind: "I wonder what other people do at 11:00pm on Saturday night?" I was so far out of touch with normal reality that I could only speculate and envy them a bit.

Day 6. Visiting Day finally arrived. I had intended to spend three hours at the treatment center with TJ, but was wonderfully surprised when he mischievously suggested we escape and go home for a few hours. I felt like Bonnie Parker driving the getaway car with my Clyde Barrow. At home, we made love, ate a pizza in bed, and watched a movie. It was heaven. For three hours, we pretended that we were carefree lovers on a tryst.

Day 7. Today I discovered that I have a very low tolerance for loneliness. Before I met and married TJ, I went out a lot: dancing, parties, lunches, and innocent mischief. I didn't have time to be bored or lonely with all the commotion. I once told my oldest daughter Amber to inscribe on my tombstone: "She Caused A Commotion." Recently, I've told her to sum up my life in these three words: "She Created Peace." But I must be honest. Peace can be colorless and loneliness stinks.

Day 8. 7/4. Independence Day. TJ told me that he was impressed with a lecture he attended in treatment about being free to make good choices. When someone is addicted to a drug like alcohol, the drug is the decision-maker, not the person. He liked the idea of being free.

Meanwhile back at the homestead, I became obsessed with researching my ancestry on the Internet. With both parents gone, I felt this urgent need to preserve the family history. I had designated myself as the official family historian and storyteller. However, it did take my breath away when I found my parents' names in the Social Security Death Index. They must really be dead after all.

Day 9. 7/5. Today I discovered that this old girl still has some spunk and spontaneity left in her after all. I got teased quite a bit by my friends for breaking my husband out of treatment for a quickie and a pizza. It may have been a reckless action by many people's standards, but it made me vibrate with life. So shoot me. I have no remorse. Today I also discovered that I have a great capacity for self-pity. I am surprised to see how often I feel sorry for myself and for my set of circumstances. Fortunately, the pitiful feelings are fleeting. They peck me like a voracious vulture then they quickly fly off in search of meatier carcasses.

Day 10. 7/6. TJ called and asked me to come pick up his guitar at the treatment center. He was upset that another patient had used it and scratched its flawless surface. As I drove up to the entrance, TJ was waiting for me outside. Beside him were the guitar case and his luggage.

"What's going on?" I gasped. "Did they kick you out?"

TJ grinned like a sly elf. "No. They changed me to outpatient status. From now on I'll come here all day, but can sleep at home at night," he added excitedly.

"Oh thank God!" I blurted out. Apparently, my prayers had been heard and my wish granted.

The first thing we did when we got home was strip down to our naked selves, and make love to each other. Everything was all right.

Day 11. 7/7. Today is my stillborn son, Jesse's, nineteenth birthday. Over the years, he has become our family's saint and protector. If he hadn't lived and died, I would never have helped create an international support center for bereaved parents. I often wondered over the years if he was an enlightened being who used me as his messenger. I'm one lucky mother.

To help me with my genealogy search, my brother, Garry, sent me the birth and death certificates of our paternal family members. They included my mom, my dad, my grandmother, my grandfather, my aunt (who was also an alcoholic), and my uncle (who was killed at age 28 by a drunk driver). My grandfather Thomas' certificate of death seized my attention. He was born in 1897 and died in 1964. He was only 67 years old. The cause of death was "Hepatic failure and coma due to Cirrhosis." Other significant conditions were cancers in three areas of his body.

Suddenly I was ten again. I was with my dad at my grandfather's home, watching him help Grandpa get in and out of bed, wash up, get dressed, and eat. My grandfather's stomach was swollen like a nine-month pregnancy due to cirrhosis of the liver, and his voice box had been removed due to cancer of the larynx. I was deeply disturbed by the appalling sight of him. After such a visit, my dad would always say to me, "See what happens when you drink and smoke too much." In a small voice I would make this big statement to my father: "I promise I'll never drink or smoke."

I showed the death certificate to TJ and pointed out the cause of death. "See why I worry so much about you," I said. He quietly nodded. "I see."

Day 12. 7/8. I just found the book, *Grandchildren of Alcoholics*. My assignment from Nancy was to read it before I started my Children of Alcoholics and Co-dependents Group on July 14th.

Day 13. 7/9 I read the first half of *Grandchildren of Alcoholics*, and was surprised how little I identified with the other grandchildren's stories in the book. The only characteristic that I had in common with them was my propensity for saving people. Two saviors raised me, so I considered it normal to save needy people. Actually, I thought that saving people was a charitable act, not a co-dependent one. I'm starting to think that Mother Teresa was co-dependent. So were Jesus and every other human being that has the title "Saint" before his or her name.

Day 14. 7/10. Family Week. It all started with a lecture on the nature of alcoholism. Then four families met in a therapy group to discuss how the behavior of our alcoholic loved ones had affected us. Later the four patients, including TJ, joined the group to hear what their family members had to say. It was agonizing for me to witness such raw emotion and suffering.

When it was my turn to confront TJ, I said that his behavior made me feel afraid, unsafe, invalidated, and unloved. The feelings bubbled up and fled out my mouth before I had a chance to censor them. My hope was that my words would not blow through his mind like wind through a screen. My hope was that they would sink in. During this session, he admitted to me that he spent an estimated $400,000.00 using alcohol and drugs since he was thirteen years old. Talk about pissing away your money.

Day 15. 7/11. Today is Mom's birthday. I wondered what she was thinking, up there above this world so high like a diamond in the sky. The second day of Family Week was just as heavy as the first. But this time, the patients were instructed to repeat to their family members what they were told the day before. They were also allowed to offer explanations. This exchange was very cathartic.

Day 16. 7/12. Today I discovered that it was time for forgive my alcoholic grandfathers. I never realized how dramatically their addictions had influenced my upbringing. The resentment that I held towards them was for the pain that they caused my parents by not attempting to recover. I accepted the facts that help was not readily available in the early sixties, and that seeking help was commonly viewed as disgraceful. My heart softened. I decided to re-read a book my grandfather Thomas wrote, and maybe write him a letter.

Day 17. 7/13. I dreamt that two brothers were each attempting to win my heart. Stubbornly, I resisted both of them, even though I knew that they were both millionaires. I guess I just wanted my TJ

This last day of Family Week was on relapse, what it was, and how to prevent it. Bottom line was that people relapse because they forget the pain they suffered and caused when they were drinking. Never lose touch with the memory of this pain was the message.

To top off this last day, TJ presented me with a shiny medallion, much like the ones he had earned in the past. He also gave a little speech, acknowledging me before God and everyone there. I felt proud and humbled. Never before had he given me an ounce of credit for sticking by him or helping him until that moment. I felt validated and deeply cherished. It was as if we had renewed our wedding vows.

Day 18. 7/14. Today is my birthday. I'm forty-seven years old. I attended my first group session, facilitated by my counselor Nancy. She commented on how much I'd changed and progressed since she had seen me two weeks before. There were six women in this group. I listened to them tell their stories, and they listened to mine. The hour dragged on. I didn't particularly like this group therapy, but I could tell that the other women did. They seemed genuinely happy when they left. I wondered what was wrong with me. All I felt was out of place.

Today, TJ officially "graduated" from rehab. They presented him with a new medallion, and sent him off into the real world. It was all so anticlimactic. I crossed my fingers, hoping that this would be his last stint at a chemical dependency rehabilitation center. Perhaps this fourth time would be a charm.

A week later, TJ and I moved into our new home. The knots in my stomach, the back of my neck, and in my vocal chords had been loosened. Now I knew I had the power, the will, and the courage to untie them.

14
THESE THINGS I LEARNED

October 2001

CREATING SOMETHING WONDERFUL

And they lived hopefully ever after. It's been nearly two years since New Year's Eve 2000 when my husband and I made the conscience decision to heal our selves and our marriage. In order to achieve these goals, we had to change our minds about a lot of big and small things, change our ways, be willing to put the past away, and be passionate about creating a new normal life together. Here's a brief update.

I suppose you're wondering how TJ is doing. I'll let him update you on his recovery.

TJ writes; "First of all, I would like to say that I'd be happy if only one person, who reads this book, benefits from my story. If that happens, then I'll feel that airing my "dirty laundry" would have been worth it.

As a boy growing up I had many rules that were given to me by my parents. (Great parents, by the way.) But I do attribute my rebellious ways to having such strict rules enforced. I remember turning eighteen and thinking, 'Now I can do anything I want to.' And I did do anything I wanted to for many years, including drinking every day. By age twenty, I already knew I was an alcoholic.

When I was twenty-three, I moved to Houston, Texas, and worked in clubs as a disc jockey. For the next nine years, I had no one around to tell me what to do or how to live. So I lived it up my way. I was definitely not embarrassed by my behavior; in fact I surrounded myself with other people who were also living the same lifestyle. I slept during the day, worked Wednesdays through Saturdays in bars, where I could drink for free on the job, and then partied on my days off.

I've come a long way since those wild days, and I feel more comfortable in my skin than I ever have before. Although I still consider myself an addict, I have found peace with myself and with my wife, mostly because of her efforts to change with me. If I hadn't married her, I might be dead by now.

Since January 2000, I have been committed to my sobriety, although it hasn't been smooth sailing. In June 2000, I relapsed big time and chose to enter rehab for help. Since then, I have continued to relapse about every six months. During my relapses I drink for one or two days, get very, very sick afterwards, and then resume my recovery. I hope someday that I'll achieve permanent sobriety, but with a disease like alcoholism, there are no such guarantees.

You might be disappointed to learn about my relapses. But I'm asking you to think about it this way: Six months is the longest time I've ever gone without drinking since I was thirteen years old and took my first drink. This is big progress for me.

Once I saw an episode of "The Simpsons" where Homer decided to get sober. He attended his first A.A. meeting. But when they told him that he would never be able to have another beer for the rest of his life, he jumped out the window right through the glass. Some days I still feel like Homer ready to jump, but most days I feel comfortable."

I can't say that I am happy when TJ relapses, but I am proud of his overall recovery. I've learned how to handle his relapses without relapsing myself. This is big progress for me, too.

TJ's second Harley-Davidson motorcycle roared into our lives last spring. Officially, it is a 2001 chrome yellow Dyna Low Ryder. This new bike is bigger and louder than the first one. He named it "Tweety" and affectionately calls it his "other blonde." On weekends we ride together on charity runs and fun runs. Riding is still a symbol of recovery for TJ, and maybe even for me, too.

My brothers and I eventually settled the negligence suit against the city over the circumstances surrounding my dad's death. They paid up, but never apologized. To my knowledge, no changes were ever made in the facility to prevent another such tragic mistake.

In April 2001, I lost another friend to alcoholism. Phil was only forty-four years old. I worked with him for many years, and his electric grin and sparkling eyes never failed to make me smile. He was tall, dark, handsome, educated, and cultured. From the outside, he appeared to be a prince. But the problem was on the inside. He admitted to me on a number of occasions that he was an alcoholic, but never chose to recover. Phil said that he knew more than the people at A.A. did, so he couldn't go there for help.

Phil was found dead in his bed. The coroner said he had been dead for three weeks before he was found. What a sad ending. The prince never kissed his princess, rode a white steed, or saved the kingdom. Perhaps in his next lifetime...

Also in April, my daughter, Noelle, became engaged to a fine gentleman, named Matt. When I heard the wonderful news, I rushed to the telephone to tell my mother. Then I remembered—Mom's dead. My heart sank and I began to cry. For a few minutes, I felt like a pitiful, motherless child. I would like to say that it's all okay because Mom is with me in spirit—but that catch phrase is not always a comfort. The truth is that it's damn hard to live without your mother and your father. If your parents are still alive, please cherish them.

I have now accepted my role of matriarch of my family. Actually, I am getting quite good at it. If I am ever in doubt about how to handle a given situation, or wonder what advice to give, I pause a moment, and ask myself, "What would Mom do or say?" Her memory is my touchstone. I have also come to believe that a person doesn't truly become an adult until both of his or her parents have died.

As I continue to recover from secondhand alcoholism, I realize how much I have changed on a very deep level. I changed my way of thinking, my way of reacting to outside stimulus, and my way of relating to myself and to others. Today, I am happy, at peace, in love with my mate, hopeful, and fully functioning.

Next month we will celebrate our eight-year wedding anniversary. Is our marriage now perfect? It's perfect for us. TJ and I laugh a lot together. We somehow came to trust each other. There are no hidden agendas, no hidden bottles, and no hidden resentments. No topic is taboo. We never go to sleep angry at each other. We choose our battles carefully. We're not too proud to extend an apology to each other, even if we think we are blameless. When things get heated, we stop and ask ourselves, "Do I want to be right or happy?" Moreover, we are committed to serenity, sanity, and simplicity.

I'm also very happy to report that my children, who didn't like or accept their stepfather for many years, now consider him a dear friend. In turn, TJ has come to love his stepchildren. In the early days of our marriage, he used to refer to them as "those kids." Now he calls them "our kids." More progress. They have great fun together, and I cannot really describe how good that makes me feel. We are a real family now.

As far as I can see into the future, Lord Alcohol and I will continue our strange dance. Every villain needs a do-gooder. That's my role, I suppose. Very few days go by when I don't encounter someone who is addicted, or is close to someone who is. Their suffering reminds me of how mine used to be. At those times, I remember the advice I was given on the final day of TJ's rehab program: "Never forget the pain." The relapse rate is high for those who forget.

I'd like to forget, but that apparently isn't what I am destined to do. I feel deep down that I am fated to remember, to speak about this horrendously unspeakable disease, and to offer a drop of comfort and hope to those who are afflicted or impacted by it. As long as there are angels, saints, and dearly departed watching my back, and God/Goddess on my mind, I will continue this dance with the dark prince.

And through it all, I learned some important life lessons by chance, not by design. Here they are.

I learned that I am not powerless over alcohol.

With apologizes to Bill Wilson, the founder of A.A., I came to realize that I was not powerless over alcohol. Before my recovery, it never occurred to me that I had the innate power to be *unaffected* by other people's alcohol use. I grew up believing that alcohol hurt people, so I allowed myself to hurt by it, not knowing that I had options.

Power is one of those controversial words. How many people do you know that describe themselves as powerful? Are you powerful? In our world, as it is, the ones who do are often found in the political arenas, in the armed forces, in gangs, or in prisons. When I studied the martial arts, the motto in my karate school was "Might for Right." We would shout it out in unison, and we actually believed that using your might or power for a good cause was all right.

I think that our founding fathers must have had a similar mind set when they slaughtered the Native Americans to build a greater America. That kind of power is actually force. It's forcing your will upon others. It's a bully mentality.

Wouldn't it be ideal to live in a world where using our might against another creature was never right?

Recovering people feel far from powerful, at least in the early stages. They've either been made to feel powerless by their own addiction, or by someone else's addiction. Where does personal power come from?

This is what medical intuitive, Caroline Myss, wrote about power in her book, *Anatomy of the Spirit*: "Power is at the root of the human experience. Our attitudes and belief patterns, whether positive or negative, are all extensions of how we define, use, or do not use power. Not one of us is free from power issues. We may be trying to cope with feelings of inadequacy or powerlessness, or we may be trying to maintain control over people or situations that we believe empower us, or we may be trying to maintain a sense of security (a synonym for power) in personal relationships. Many people who lose something that represents power to them—money, or a job, or a game—or who lose someone in whom their sense of self or power is vested—a spouse or lover, a parent or child—develop a disease. Our relationship to power is at the core of our health."

If you are one of those people who think that all power comes from God, then for Heaven's sake, request more of it. If you think that it comes from within, call it up to the surface. If you think it comes from a magic talisman or visiting a sacred site, then go for it. Whatever it takes, as long as the activity harms no one, do it.

I learned that both peace and suffering are choices.

The Buddha revealed many centuries ago that the true cause of suffering is non-acceptance. For me, choosing to accept, but not necessarily like, seemingly unacceptable situations and people, has eased and even prevented much personal suffering. When things get tense, as they often do, I now pause and consider these two options before I speak or act. Do I want suffering or serenity? Do I want to be right or at peace?

There are hundreds of small choices to make each day. Some of them will create suffering, and some will create serenity. I can affect the outcome by choosing the tone of my voice, my next remark, my facial expression, and even my next emotion. Yes, emotions are choices, too. I have the power to choose to be sad, mad, glad, or fearful. I can also consciously choose the type of music, colors, movies, food, television programs, clothing, books, work, and relationships that promote serenity.

However, I must say that choosing the path of serenity is tough sometimes. Being warrioress at heart, my initial response to a threat or fear is to stand up and fight, which inevitably creates suffering. Some days, choosing a peaceful response requires the help of at least four archangels. No, I am not saint. I admit that I still sometimes barge like a mad cow down Suffering Highway, but not as often as I used to.

On most days, I even find myself pausing to notice the moments of sheer contentment and serenity that I have created; something I don't remember doing before my recovery. These are holy moments.

I came to love the Serenity Prayer. "God grant me the serenity to accept the things I cannot change, the courage to change the things I can, and the wisdom to know the difference." This prayer is so simple, yet so meaty. To accept the unacceptable and still be all right reveals the deepest truth of the Universe, in my humblest opinion. Serenity is heaven on earth.

I learned that I am what I think I am.

My motto is "I am not what you think I am. I am what I think I am." As a society, we tend to label things--canned goods, clothing, even people. Personally, I have been tagged with an assortment of labels in my lifetime-- mother, wife, Irish, Minnesotan, author, the blonde, the black belt, and sometimes the witch and the bitch. Some people like labels. Just ask a devoted Trekkie or groupie. But some people don't. As I've said before, I never liked being labeled "co-dependent." It makes me cringe. It feels wrong. It belittles me.

I know that I am not co-dependent. I just happened, by luck or karma, to marry an alcoholic. From what I have read, co-dependents have three main characteristics: 1. They are greatly and negatively affected by an addict's behavior. 2. They attempt to control people and situations. 3. They obsess about the addict.

As always, I have a few things to say about these so-called negative characteristics. First, I believe that we all are directly or indirectly affected by the people we are close to. What mother is not affected by her baby's chronic crying spells or her teenager's pierced nose, tongue, or belly button? If we were not affected, what is the point of being in relationship with anyone or anything? Being affected is a good thing.

Second, I think that attempting to control our personal world is also normal and necessary. It is called self- and tribal-preservation. I assume that a person becomes co-dependent when their controlling becomes obsessive. Although, I do think that being obsessive about certain things is good, too. What great politician, artist, scientist, mystic, or poet wasn't obsessed with his or her personal goal?

Finally, I have found that obsessing about the addict's behavior is futile. I can barely control my own behavior let alone the actions of another. The only way to cure this tendency is to learn how to control your thoughts, and to become aware of your thoughts while your thinking them. If they are positive thoughts, keep them. If not, send them packing. When I find myself caught in a conundrum of obsessive thoughts, I meditate with the sole intention of stopping all thoughts from passing through my mind. I am able to accomplish this by focusing on nothing except my breathing. Soon, my mind is empty, and I can restock its shelves with fresh food for thought.

To me, co-dependency is not a disease. It's a bad habit. It's an unbalanced way of thinking and reacting to outside forces. It starts out all innocent and benign, but after a while, this way of thinking and reacting becomes a habit and then a lifestyle. Then you're in deep shit. My suggestion here: Avoid becoming the labels that are sometimes stuck on you.

I learned that not everyone is a group person.

What a funny world we live in. In America, there is a support group for everything, and I mean everything, that troubles you. Misery certainly loves company. And some of these groups are helpful, no doubt. But wouldn't it be wonderful to have a group for people who think that life is great? Author Marianne Williamson suggested that there be a support group for people who are just fine. *"Hello. My name is Susan. I'm happy, good-looking, rich, and thin."* What a fabulous idea.

I came to realize (to my counselor's dismay) that I didn't like support groups. I tried bereavement groups, Al-Anon meetings, Co-dependent groups, and Adult Children of Alcoholics groups, but I felt as out of sync in them as a cat trying to bark. Some people, like my husband, are group people. But some people, like me, are not. Are you a group person? If you're not sure, I suggest that you give few self-help groups a good and true try. If they aren't for you, find another source of support and comradery.

Try a health club, a dance studio, a spiritual group, a charity, a new job, or a team sport. But first, I suggest that you seek support from your family members. Before this age of support groups, people found advice and solace within the arms of their family members. What a novel idea.

I learned that addictions aren't all bad.

It's ironic, but after some time I began to see that addictions also have a good side. We all have some little addictions or attachments. Even His Holiness the Dalai Lama, the reigning detachment expert, admitted to becoming attached to pets in the monastery. Little attachments seem to be okay as long as they harm no one, including yourself. But from what I have seen so far, I believe that big addictions can be either catastrophic or enlightening. They can maim and kill some people, or they can awaken people to their truest spiritual nature.

I love to hear stories about people who rose up from the deep end of their rock-bottom addictions, got well somehow, and lived awe-inspiring lives thereafter. I especially like the story, the life, and the work of the contemporary artist, Andy Lakey. He was a heavy-duty cocaine addict, who had a near-death experience that changed his life dramatically.

Before his overdose, he was a used car salesman. Afterwards, inspired by a heavenly vision during his "death", he devoted his life to painting angels. Today, he is one of the world's foremost painters of angels and art for the blind, and his works hang in museums, churches, hospitals, and homes worldwide. To learn more about Andy Lakey and his art, I urge you to visit his breath-taking web site: www.andylakey.com.

The point I'm clumsily trying to make is that without Andy's addiction, there would be no angel art to inspire and illuminate us. Imagine what you could do if you could see the flip side of your addictions.

I learned that human beings should not drink alcohol--ever.

The last time I checked, alcohol wasn't the fifth basic food group, although you'd never know it by the speed in which some people lap it up. I hate to be the one to say it, but human bodies were not made to consume alcohol. If they were, then drinking alcohol would promote good health, not monstrous headaches, hangovers, liver disease, addiction, insanity, and death.

I came to know, without a doubt, that *no human being* should drink alcohol. No one. The risks far, far outweigh the momentary benefits, such as temporary relief from problems and stress, comradery, or synthetic fun. I'm for voluntary sobriety for all.

I learned that forgiveness is next to Godliness.

Saints forgive. Humans hold a grudge. That's what I used to think. What I have found to be true is that forgiveness is an excellent choice if you want to be happy. Choices, choices, and more choices.

Even though I had to drag myself to the moment, I eventually did forgive my husband for the pain that he, whether intentional or not, inflicted on me during his drinking career. Contrary to what I used to think, forgiving him did not weaken me, but rather it strengthened me, and it strengthened my relationship with him.

Forgiving someone doesn't mean you approve of their actions. It also doesn't mean you have to like the person, or ever speak to the person again. Moreover, the person doesn't even need to know that they're forgiven. All that counts is that you know.

I highly recommend forgiveness. It's a selfish thing to do. It makes you feel better. It lightens your load. It prepares you for better things to come, sort of like tilling barren soil. Soon after, new life springs forth, like shoots of sweet grass.

I learned that, when in doubt, take the Middle Way.

The Buddha promoted the benefits of the Middle Way or the middle path. Taking the middle path, instead of extreme lefts or rights, can help people create a life of calm detachment, by which the wise person avoids extremes of self-indulgence and austerity. Just follow the yellow brick road…

The Buddha once gave the example of a musician who tries to play his instrument with strings that are strung too tightly or too loosely. Without adjusting the strings to a point somewhere in the middle of these two extremes, it is impossible to create beautiful music. He said that the same is true for our spiritual life; it should neither be too slack, nor stretched to the breaking point. But somewhere in the middle lies the harmony.

I think that Americans, especially, are rather extreme people. We have a propensity for over-eating, over-spending, over-working, and even over-playing. "More is better" appears to be the American philosophy of life. But this tendency to over-do is apparently taking its toll, resulting in a fat, addicted, broke, stressed out, and sick population. And it's easy to get sucked into this lifestyle. Buy more, do more, be more. More, more, more. But look around. Has this more mentality shaped us into a peaceful, happy race? Quite the opposite.

"When in doubt, choose the Middle Way" is my new motto. However, to avoid extremes takes a degree of discipline, along with a keen desire for peace and harmony, personally, tribally, and globally. Each decision made in a course of a day or a lifetime moves us either down the middle path, to the far right, or to the far left.

Personally, I have found that when I have strayed from the middle path, I became physically sick or emotionally unbalanced. My body lets me know in no uncertain terms when I have made extreme decisions, such as getting too little or too much sleep, exercise, food, or stress management. My body will give me warning signals, like headaches, stomachaches, backaches, colds, or worse, if I refuse to correct my course.

I learned that love is not all you need.

I used to have the romantic notion that if I loved the addict enough, he would be cured. I thought that love was the answer to every dilemma. And it probably is in the very, very broadest sense. But when it comes to curing an addict, I have come to believe that willingness is more necessary than love in the early stages of recovery.

Hard core addicts are not emotionally connected. They can comprehend love intellectually, but often not feel it. Feelings come later once their recovery has progressed a bit. I foolishly thought that my husband would be motivated to become well out of love for me, for his family, or for himself. I thought I could love him into submission. But what I didn't understand at the time was that Lord Alcohol had blocked or destroyed his feelings of love.

Willingness, in my opinion, is the miracle cure for all ills. If an ill person is truly willing to become well, he or she has set the miracle of healing in motion. I have heard that when a doctor tells a patient that he has cancer, the patient decides in the first fifteen seconds, following the announcement, whether or not he will live or die. The patient decides. How? He decides with his thoughts. He will either become willing to be healed or willing to die. Two opposite choices. I believe that the same theory applies to addicted people. They decide, often during a rock bottom moment, to either become healed or to die. The addict's partner must also be willing to change, and willing to become happy and healthy. Where there's a will…

I learned that help comes in a variety of shapes and sizes.

Some of my most effective caregivers were not doctors, priests, or psychologists. They were psychics, hypnotists, authors, and monks.

I came to see how very difficult it is to recover without the support of professionals and loved ones. Very few people recover alone. But at our worst, we do feel totally alone. We need help and don't know where to find it. We probably don't even know what kind of help we need. All you need to know is that help will arrive if you ask for it. Who do you ask? Ask a friend, family member, or co-worker. Call a professional. Drop in at a support group. Or pray. Remember, angels don't swoop in unless they're asked.

I do understand that for some people it is hard to ask for help from anyone, least of all from God. Some of us are stuck on the idea that we are totally self-sufficient. But that's just a lie we tell ourselves. The truth is that we need each other; that's the nature of the human experience.

If it's hard for you to ask others for help, then your life will be harder than it could be.

If you are unwilling to accept the help that is offered to you, then you will find that many unacceptable experiences await you.

Try this. If you are currently unable to ask for or accept the help of others, then offer help to others instead. Hold a door open for someone, give another driver your parking space, donate to a good cause, or give a needy person the cash in your pocket. Helping others makes you feel good. Why not let others experience the joy of helping you, too?

I learned to see myself as the creator of my life.

I came to know that I am the creator of my own life. I am the artist. Although God created me, I don't think that He has any particular agenda for how my life should unfold. He gave each of us free will, and wants us to use it. He is not the Grand Puppeteer; pulling our strings, and making us do this or that. I think that He just looks on and loves us, like a parent who has let go of his or her grown children. Wise parents know that they can't live their children's lives for them, they can't save them, and they can't control them, no matter how hard they try. So why try?

Q: What is the tool of creation? A: Your thoughts. "As you think, so shall you be."

As the creator of my life, I can paint my life with broad strokes, thin lines, bold colors, or dark shadows. It's my choice, my illusion, and my work of art. It's your choice, too. You can become a never-was or one singular sensation. It's entirely up to you. You can accept full credit and full blame. You can change what needs changing. There is no such thing as adding too much love or too much beauty to your creation. You are the master painter and the masterpiece. And when you have finished your project, tuck it away in a closet, and begin again with a fresh canvas. Reincarnate.

I learned to cultivate friendships in High Places.

Adversity has motivated me to have many friends in High Places. Some of these "unseen friends" are God, Goddess, angels, spirit guides; deceased loved ones, nature spirits, muses, and even some E.T.s. These are real friendships with real beings, which have taken a special interest in me or my work, and I in theirs. We share ideas, experiences, insights, and emotions. I value their perspective, as they can see life from both sides of the veil.

You might be wondering how a human can have a friendship with a spirit. It's easy and natural. To begin, you must desire such contact and then be willing to learn how to become more aware of their presence in your daily life. Although I think it's rare to have a spirit materialize before you, most spirit friends will communicate with you in whatever way you'll accept. Mostly, I think that they impress their thoughts upon your mind.

You might have a feeling that someone non-physical is in the room. It might be a strange thought or great idea that suddenly pops into your head, a whisper in your ear, a distinct scent, an odd light in the room, or a gentle touch on your shoulder. The contact could happen in a night dream, a daydream, during prayer or meditation, while you're in the shower, driving your car, or washing dishes. The more you go into "the gap" or at least observe a time of silence each day; the easier the contact will be. Often, I will feel my mother at my side, or my angel peering over my shoulder as I write. Mentally, I communicate with them.

Most humans do have a relationship, but not necessarily a friendship, with the Great Spirit. Having a friendship with God can be an incomprehensible idea for many people, who view God as unapproachable, judgmental, or even vindictive. But views, like diapers, need to be changed sometimes. If you truly desire to have a friendlier relationship with God, read the stunning book, *Friendship with God*, by best-selling author, Neale Donald Walsch. Warning! This book is not for the narrow-minded or change-resisters.

I learned to have and show compassionate towards those who suffer.

I came to have compassion for the sorrow and suffering of addicts. Prior to my own recovery, I viewed addicts as very hopeless, weak people. It's one thing to have compassion, and decidedly another thing to show it. So don't hesitate to show it. Every act of kindness and compassion counts. Every kiss, every hug, every hello, every prayer, every smile touches someone, somewhere, somehow.

His Holiness the Dalai Lama has stated: "For as long as space endures, and for as long as living beings remain, until then may I, too, abide to dispel the misery of the world." We, who have taken this recovery voyage, can be lighthouses to others adrift on the deep, dark sea of life. Shine on!

I learned the value of acknowledging the heroes in my life.

This world needs more heroes. The dictionary describes a hero as "A person noted for feats of courage or nobility of purpose, especially one who has risked or sacrificed his or her life." Unfortunately, in our society we tend to only make heroes out of actors, athletes, and comic strip characters, failing to notice the real, unsung heroes and heroines in our lives.

Who are the heroes in your life?

If you need to meet a real live hero, try attending an A.A. meeting at your local church or community center. I know you'll find some great people there, performing acts of heroism. They might be driving a former drunk to meetings, because she had her driver's license revoked, or raising the spirits of a fellow member who recently received divorce papers or lost custody of his children. They might be quietly praying for those at the meeting who would kill (or have killed) for a drink of Lord Alcohol. These heroes call strangers by name, share their darkest secrets in order to light someone else's path, and draw their swords of serenity to ward off evil spirits. Every month or so, I attend an A.A. meeting with my husband. It keeps me humble and the heroes there inspire me.

TJ is one of my heroes. I am in awe of his feats of courage; slaying his dragon, overcoming unimaginable obstacles, and continually battling a disease that has no cure, no clear cut course of treatment, and no conscience. And doing all this with humor, panache, and the guts of forty thieves. That's a hero, in my book. Bravo, TJ!

I came to know that "sober fun" is not an oxymoron.

You may not believe me, but you can have fun without drinking alcohol. It's true. TJ and I had to find new, fun things to do, far away from alcohol. Initially, we kept frequenting our favorite places, where we used to dance and have fun, but it never worked out well for us. He'd end up tempted to drink, and I'd end up mad at him. We had to change our social habits.

Today, we seldom accept invitations to events that we know will include a lot of drinking, like weddings, tailgating parties, happy hours, some concerts, and all bars. We gave up dancing in clubs, which was a sacrifice. Eventually, we did find fun sober things to do. Here are a few suggestions:

- Invite people to your home to watch sports events, instead of going to sports bars.

- Dance at a dance studio instead of at nightclubs. Although TJ and I no longer dance in clubs, we still dance together in amateur productions, like in "The Nutcracker" last Christmas at my daughter Amber's dance studio.
- Instead of attending gatherings like weddings that you know will include alcohol, either send your regrets, or go early before the free booze is flowing like unholy water. Weddings can be an alcoholic's paradise.

- Take up a new hobby. We joined a Harley Owners Group (HOG) in St. Paul, Minnesota with 1100 members. They offer weekly runs to various scenic sites, or rides to benefit charities. If they stop at a bar, we wait outside and chat with other riders about their bikes.

- Create your own web site. Make it a showplace for family photos, or perhaps an educational or entertaining site for others.

- Explore your genealogy. It's fun to discover your roots and share that information with other family members.

- Take a brisk walks or bicycle rides around a nearby lake or through a park.

- Plan regular picnics, even if the weather is lousy. Sometimes I spread a checkered tablecloth over our bed and hold our picnic there.

- Go horseback riding, take a vacation, take up miniature golf, join a health club, take a yoga class, or feed the ducks in the park.

- Attend charitable events, such as walks, runs, concerts, or dances. Usually, these events are booze-less.

15
LIFE WITHOUT ALCOHOL

6 HEALTHY REASONS NOT TO DRINK

"If your objective is to live a life of good health and great longevity, consuming dead flesh, smoking known carcinogens, and drinking volumes of nerve-deadening, brain-frying liquids *does not work*. This has already been demonstrated, " writes Neale Donald Walsch in *Conversations with God*, Book 3.

About two-thirds of all adults drink alcohol. People use alcohol for a variety of cultural, religious, medical, social, and personal reasons. It is so commonly used that most people forget that it's a drug, a legal, highly addictive, openly used drug.

There is an old saying that goes something like this: Drinking two drinks a day makes you healthy. Drinking three a day makes you an alcoholic. If there is any truth to this adage, then the line between healthy and addicted is a very fine one. (A drink is 1 ½ ounces of 80-proof or 1 ounce of 100-proof whiskey, 5 ounces of wine, or 12 ounces of regular or light beer.)

This chapter spells out the benefits of not drinking alcoholic beverages. It was not written for alcoholics or alcohol-dependent people. It was written for the average Joe or Jane, who are interested in making healthy lifestyle choices. Regular exercise, good nutrition, and stress management are the undoubtedly the basic Level 1 activities necessary for healthy living. Vegetarianism, alternative healing methods, smoking cessation, and meditation appear to be Level 2 methods. I realize this is radical, but I am inviting you to step up to Level 3, which is simply not to drink any alcoholic beverages.

Human bodies were obviously not intended to digest alcohol, which is why alcohol consumption produces such negative outcomes. If someone will prove to me without a doubt that consuming alcohol has any indisputably beneficial qualities, I will reconsider my stand.

Here are six good reasons not to drink. Maybe one or two of them will hit home with you.

REASON 1: Drinking harms your body.

Alcoholism is a major public health problem. Drinking promotes heart disease, cancer, liver disorders, gastrointestinal problems, infections, skin, muscle, and bone disorders, hormonal imbalances, diabetes, malnutrition, and respiratory problems. When consumed during pregnancy, it causes fetal alcohol syndrome.

Drinking alcohol ages your body prematurely. Let's be honest. Consummate drinkers are easy to spot. Their eyes are bloodshot and their noses and cheeks are discolored from broken blood vessels. They look old and haggard. It is not a pretty sight. Alcohol is also high in calories. Where do you think the term "beer belly" came from?

Drinking alcohol can interfere with your sleep, disturbing the crucial REM sleep stage and preventing dreams, which are vital to good health.

Drinking alcohol causes some people to become addicted to it. Alcohol is an addictive drug. Even when drinking only one drink per day, a person can become physically and/or psychologically dependent on the drug. Alcohol and marijuana have also been found to be gateway drugs, which lead to other drug use, such as cocaine, heroine, crack, etc.

Drinking alcohol shortens your life. Heavy drinkers shorten their life spans by 10 to 12 years. In recent years, some medical studies have indicated that one drink of alcohol a day has health benefits. However, these reported benefits are limited only to adults over 60 years old who have risks for heart disease. As people age, it takes fewer drinks to become intoxicated, and organs can be damaged easier than in younger drinkers. Drinking can also lead to accidental death and suicide. In 80 percent of suicides, the victim had been drinking.

REASON 2: Drinking harms your mind.

Your ability to make sound and sane decisions can be impaired when you drink. Alcohol initially acts on the parts of your brain, which affects self-control, and other learned behaviors. Less than two drinks can impair some people's ability to drive a car, find their car keys, or find their way home from the pub or party.

Drinking kills brain cells. All those dead brain cells result in memory loss, slowed thinking and reactions, physical degeneration, and even slurred speech when sober.

Drinking alcohol also causes temporary amnesia, impairing your ability to remember events. It surprises me how many very important decisions are made while people are under the influence of alcohol, like business deals, marriages, conceptions, major purchases, and sexual interludes. Alcohol can also make some people temporarily forget about the most important people and things in their lives: their children, their spouses, their homes, their careers, their values, and their money. The result of this alcohol-induced amnesia has ruined many good men, women, and children.

REASON 3: Drinking hinders your spiritual growth.

Spirit and drinking spirits don't mix well. People who drink as a way to relax and forget life's problems, for the most part, do not develop a close relationship with themselves, with others, or with God. By the time addicts finally reach rock bottom and are ready to seek professional help, they are generally quite spiritually bankrupt. (I think of spirituality as your relationship with God, and not about adhering to a certain set of religious beliefs.)

One of the goals of A.A. is to reconnect them with "a power greater than themselves." I'm not sure why alcohol keeps people separated from God. Maybe it's because a person can't successful serve two masters.

If you don't feel spiritually connected, there are ways to reconnect. Some of these ways are through prayer, meditation, daily reading and writing in a journal, or listening to inspiring music. Or you can spend time observing Nature, taking a retreat, attending a support group meeting, seeing God in the little things (flowers, art, kittens, babies), being grateful for all that you do have, tending a garden, spending time with a pet, or performing acts of kindness.

REASON 4: Drinking harms your reputation.

It's an interesting study to see how alcohol affects people. Sometimes they become nicer, more romantic, or less shy. But sometimes they turn into monsters, which talk loudly and incessantly about nothing, repeat themselves, stagger, fall down, make unwanted sexual advances, cry, pick fights, drool, pee in a potted plant, or strip down to their underwear. And all this might happen at a company Christmas party or a Baptism. It doesn't take too many of those incidents for a person to be labeled a drunk or worse.

Reputations can be ruined further still if the person has committed an alcohol-related offense, such as DWI, disturbing the peace, domestic disturbance, or assault while under the influence. If convicted, these charges remain permanently on your criminal record, making it impossible to get certain jobs, adopt a baby, vote, or even lease an apartment. A reputation is a terrible thing to waste.

REASON 5: Drinking harms the family.

Drinking can lead to relationship problems, which can harm the family unit. Domestic abuse is a common consequence of alcohol abuse. In 60 percent of child abuse cases, alcohol is involved.

Adultery is another byproduct of too much alcohol ingestion. Enough said.

Drinking can interfere with intimacy. It's impossible to be really close to someone who abuses alcohol. They just are never fully present in their own skin.

Drinking deadens or heightens emotions. Have you every tried to have a serious conversation with someone who is loaded? It usually turns into a shouting match, a pity party, or a war.

Drinking alcohol increases the chance that your children will also drink. I have personally witnessed a family attempt to heal from the devastating effects of having an alcoholic child. I have never seen such anguish. The couple ended up divorcing, the addicted child never did become clean and sober, and their other children acted out violently. Everyone lost.

Drinking alcohol is expensive. It robs the family unit of resources. Note the cost of beer, wine, hard liquor purchased at a liquor store or bought in a bar. Multiple that figure times 365 days, then multiply by the average life span of 80 years. Yikes. Remember, TJ's tab for twenty-eight years of career drinking totaled more than $400,000.00.

REASON 6: Drinking alcohol harms society.

Drinkers put everyone at risk. As long as they're out there, we're not as safe as we could otherwise be. It only takes one drunk driver to kill an entire family. Once I was interviewed by Candy Lightner; the founder of Mothers Against Drunk Drivers (MADD). Her daughter was killed by a drunk driver. I'll never forget Candy's devastation at the senseless loss.

Drinking alcohol increases your risk of accidents. If you or your companions have consumed alcohol in the past few hours, your chances of being involved in an accident increases. The majority of people involved in motorized vehicle and water sports accidents have been drinking alcohol. As I've mentioned before, the statistics speak for themselves: In 65 percent of reported fatal accidents, alcohol is involved.

Drinking alcohol exposes you to certain crimes. The lethal magic of alcohol is that is gives certain people the courage and confidence to act in ways that are contrary to their values. When you drink, or are close to someone who does, you increase your chances of being involved in crimes. Some of these crimes include: DWI, vehicular homicide, rape, assault, domestic abuse, road rage, theft, illegal drug use, and even murder. A high school girlfriend of mine was murdered a few years ago by a drunk boyfriend. Her children found her dead in the garage in a freezer.

"Most homicides occur between people who know each other, while under the influence of a drug, such as alcohol. (Eighty percent of the people in jail committed crimes while drugged.) Many of these convicted felons truly do not remember committing crimes," writes Toby Rice Drews in *Getting Them Sober --you can help!*

IMAGINE

Try for a moment to imagine your life without alcohol.

Q: What would you do for fun?
Q: How would you relax?
Q: How would you alter your consciousness?
Q: What would you do with the extra money?
Q: Extra time?
Q: Extra energy?
Q: How would your close relationships change?

Now try to imagine a world without alcohol. I feel a little like John Lennon asking you to envision a world so different than it is now. This is what I envision. I imagine that people would live longer, happier, and healthier lives, families would be less fragmented, the courts would be far less congested, the police would have more time for community service, and individuals would learn to solve their problems instead of hiding from them. But mostly, I like to imagine the human race becoming a spiritual race again with a deep connection to God and to one another.

I have a big secret to tell you. There are safe ways to alter your consciousness, like alcohol does, without the nasty side effects. One of these safe ways is with daily meditation. It can create euphoric feelings better and safer than any drug you can get legally or illegally. Try it. You'll like it.

16
KIDS & BOOZE

HELPING YOUR KIDS AVOID
ALCOHOL ADDICTION

Society tends to focus on teenage drinking only after a tragedy has occurred, such as a fatal car accident or a fraternity death caused by alcohol poisoning.

I am the mother of five grown children. Some of my kids drink alcohol, and some don't. They know the risks. They have free will to choose. I don't believe that there is such a thing as "responsible drinking." When you consume alcoholic beverages, you are ingesting a drug. This drug is unpredictable and dangerous.

As with smoking cigarettes, the key to not becoming addicted is never to take that first drag or sip. My son, Jake, made this statement to me when he was about seven years old: "Alcohol will never cross my lips in this lifetime." The magnitude of the declaration, and the actual wording of the statement shocked me. When I asked him what motivated his strong feelings, he said that Grandpa (my dad) warned him never to drink. Today, Jake is twenty-five-years-old, and true to his vow, has not allowed alcohol to cross his lips so far. But I think Jake is an exception to the rule. Most kids do experiment with alcohol; some become social drinkers; some become alcoholics; and some choose never to drink.

Experts think that it is easy to spot the children that are at risk of becoming heavy-duty drinkers someday. These at-risk kids have parents who drink regularly; alcohol is kept in their homes; they tend to need instant gratification; have a greater than average need for acceptance by their peers; have limited parental supervision; and/or have been diagnosed with attention deficit disorder.

This is what WebMD has to say about underage drinking: "People with a family history of alcoholism are more likely to being drinking before the age of 20 and to become alcoholic. But anyone who begins drinking in adolescence is at higher risk. Currently 1.9 million young people between the ages of 12 and 20 are considered heavy drinkers and 4.4 million are binge drinkers."

As parents, we innately wish to keep our children out of harm's way. Sometimes our efforts work; sometimes they don't. Here are a few suggestions that may help you steer your children towards an alcohol-free lifestyle.

- Don't drink alcohol yourself. Period.

- If you need help to stop drinking alcohol, seek it out immediately.

- Don't wait until after you get your first DWI. There is Alcoholic Anonymous groups and chemical dependency treatment facilities in almost every city.

- Don't keep alcohol in your home, even for company.

- Show your kids, by example, that people of all ages can have great fun without alcohol or drugs.

- Refuse to help alcohol manufacturers advertise their products by wearing their logos and slogans on your clothing or other possessions.

- Stay out of bars. Let's be real honest here: No one goes to bars just to because "everyone knows their name" there. People go to bars to drink.

- Try as much as possible to avoid activities sponsored by bars and alcohol manufacturers. Don't ask bars and liquor stores to sponsor your softball team. Buy your own tee shirts.

- Learn about the negative effects of alcohol on the human body, mind, and spirit so that you can speak intelligently about them to your children.

- Support drug and alcohol prevention programs in your community, such as DARE.

- If there is alcoholism in your family, definitely warn your children about their own possible predisposition towards the disease.

- Speak of alcoholics as sick people, not bad people.

- Donate money to those organizations that are seeking to find a cure of alcoholism and drug addiction.

- Don't forbid your children to use alcohol. People, by nature, love to do the forbidden just to break up the monotony of everyday life. Motivate by example instead. Encourage don't forbid.

- Praise your children when they choose an alcohol-free party, prom, or concert to attend.

- Learn, then teach, your children how to alter their consciousness without drugs, such as with prayer, meditation, walking, dancing, smiling, writing, and practicing loving kindness. There is no high like a meditation high.

- Instead trying to fight alcohol abuse, try making peace with it. Don't hate it; just don't make a cozy room for it in your thinking or your life.

- Lobby to have a warning label on all products containing alcohol, like the one on cigarette packs.

- Talk to your child. Find out his or her feelings about drinking alcohol. If he or she decides to drink alcohol, and they are of legal drinking age, accept it...and pray for their well-being. If they're underage, get help!

- If you suspect that your spouse or child is abusing alcohol, confront them. Ask them to get help. If they refuse (which they usually do), consider arranging an intervention. Intervention is explained in the book, *Intervention: How to Help Someone Who Doesn't Want Help*, by Vernon E. Johnson.

- Lobby to increase penalties for those selling or otherwise providing alcohol to minors.

- Feel proud of your alcohol-free lifestyle, and promote its benefits to others.

The benefits include:
A longer life span
Better physical, mental, emotional, and spiritual health
More money to save, spend or donate
Less hassles with the police, bosses, and loved ones
A greater ability to succeed in all areas of your life
Less chance of accidents, including accidental pregnancies
The privilege of having and keeping your driver's license
Less permanent brain and organ damage
Less chance that your children's children will drink
The prevention of alcoholism and drug addiction
More room in jails and prisons for real criminals
More room in our court system to hear real crimes
Less child, sexual, domestic abuse overall
Happier, healthier, and more functional people, families, and society
Less violence altogether
More inner and global peace
More time and interest in spirituality, the arts, and other activities that uplift people
Less gratuitous sex and violence on television and in the movies
More love of self and others

Parenting is not an easy job. I've been at it for twenty-seven years and am still learning how to be an effective parent. Luckily, I had two fabulous role models: my own mom and dad. May you also become the kind of parents that your children will use as role models one sweet day.

Dear Reader: It's time to go now. But before I go, I wanted for you to know that I thought about you every day when I sat down to write this story. I wondered how you were, who you were, and if I could positively impact you with my words. I worried about you. Moreover, I loved you for listening to my story--you helped heal me just by listening and I am grateful. Farewell.

ACKNOWLEDGEMENTS

I would like to thank and acknowledge those who have helped me bring this book, and this particular chapter of my life, to a happy and safe ending.

First of all, I want to acknowledge my husband, TJ Martinez. Even though I was an unwilling student, he managed to teach me volumes about love and healing. And I thought I knew it all before I met him. This has probably been one of the most exhausting lifetimes we have spent together, but also the most enlightening. Maybe some day we'll really be able to see in the dark. You're my hero! I also want to thank his parents for creating such a masterpiece.

To my children, Amber, Jake, Noelle, Luke, and Rachael Erling. I want to thank you for choosing me as your mother in this lifetime. Even during my dark night of the soul, I could always see your five love lights burning for me. Thank you for that. Each of one of you is like a rare jewel, sparkling in the sunlight, a little rough around the edges, but breathtaking for human eyes to behold. Shine on!

To my parents, Jack and Nora Borden. I want you to know that life down here on earth is a little less colorful without you. You were the perfect parents for me. Mom praised me to success, and Dad loved me like a great lion loves his cubs. To have an unlimited supply of love and praise is every child's dream. Remember us!

To my dearest friend, Jamie McNaughton. You are the sister I never had. With three brothers, I grew up a little lonely, always wishing for a sister. Then I found you! Two blondes in cahoots can be a dangerous combination, as we have already proven. I'll never forget how hard I laughed when one time you didn't get a blonde joke that I was telling you! Keep on having more fun than everyone else!

To the members of Alcoholics Anonymous, who rushed to our sides when others pretended that they didn't hear our cries for help. You're the best. Where else on earth could we have found such support, acceptance, and friendship during a time when society viewed us as outcasts? If I wrote a book about you, the entire text would read: Thank you. Thank you. Thank you.

I also want to acknowledge TJ's care providers at Fairview Riverside Recovery Center in Minneapolis, Minnesota. I know that you were just doing your jobs, but you've got tough jobs to do. Judging by TJ's progress so far, you have made a positive impact upon him, and steered him in the right and righteous direction. The three rehabilitation programs that he attended before yours didn't seem to have even left a chink in his armor. But yours did. Thank you from the depths of my soul. Don't forget to sometimes ask yourselves, "How does that make you feel?" Keep the faith!

And finally, I'd like to thank all of the authors, who wrote the books that picked me up, that kicked my butt, and that pushed me forward when I was face down in a mud hole. Some of these mystics and magicians are Deepak Chopra, Thich Nhat Hanh, Sophy Burnham, Jack Kornfield, His Holiness the Dalai Lama, and Caroline Myss. My very favorite author is Rumi, the transcendental poet that personally delivered messages from The Great Beyond right into my heart. What would God do without writers like you?

Peace on earth.

Good will towards all men and women everywhere.

BIBLIOGRAPHY &
SUGGESTED READING LIST

Alexander, Bill, *Cool Water: Alcoholism, Mindfulness and Ordinary Recovery*, 1997

Ash, Mel, *Zen of Recovery*, Jeremy P. Tarcher/Putnam, 1993

Barks, Coleman with John Moyne (translation), *The Essential Rumi*, HarperSanFrancisco, 1995

Beattie, Melody, *Playing It by Heart: Taking care of Yourself No Matter What*, Hazelden, 1999

Beattie, Melody, *Codependent No More*, Hazelden Foundation, 1987

Brooks, Jane, *Midlife Orphan: Facing Life's Changes Now that Your Parents are Gone*, Berkley Books, 1999

Chopra, Deepak, *Overcoming Addictions: The Spiritual Solution*, Ramdom House, 1997

Dalai Lama, *The Art of Happiness: A Handbook for Living*, 1998

Drews, Toby Rice, *Getting Them Sober-- you can help!*, Recovery Communications, Inc. 1994

Hofer, Angelika and Gunter Ziesler, *The Lion Family Book*, Picture Book Studio, 1988

Kornfield, Jack, *After the Ecstasy, the Laundry*, Bantam Books, 2000

Montgomery, Ruth, *Strangers Among Us*, Fawcett Crest, 1979

Myss, Caroline, *Anatomy of the Spirit*, Three Rivers Press, 1996

Pinkola Estes, Clarissa, *Women Who Run With the Wolves*, Ballantine Books, 1992

Powter, Susan, *Sober...and Staying that Way: The Missing Link in the Cure for Alcoholism*, 1999

Ross Carter, John and Mahinda Palaihawadana (translation), *Sacred Writings, Buddhism: The Dhammapada*, The Oxford University Press, 1987

Salzberg, Sharon, *Loving-Kindness: The Revolutionary Art of Happiness*, Shambhala, 1995

Taylor, Terry Lynn, *The Alchemy of Prayer*, H.J. Kramer, 1996

Nhat Hanh, Thich, *The Long Road To Joy*, Parallax Press, 1996

Walsch, Neale Donald, *Friendship With God*, G.P. Putnam's Sons, 1999

Walsch, Neale Donald, *Conversations With God, Book 3*, G.P. Hampton Roads, 1998

ABOUT THE AUTHOR

Susan Erling Martinez is the author of many books, booklets, and articles on the topics of loss and grief, alternative healing, self-protection, and spirituality. The book titles include *Last Call for Alcohol: Healing a Marriage Harmed by Alcohol Abuse*, *Angels & Dreams: Add Sparkle to your Life with the Help of the Angels and your Dreams*, *Life-Guard: A Woman's Personal Safety Guide*, and *Safe & Sound: A Parent's Guide to Self-Protection for Kids*.

Susan is a certified hypnotherapist, holds a black belt in karate, and was a pioneer in the field of assisting people who have experienced a childbearing loss. She lives in Minnesota with her husband, TJ Martinez, and her five grown children. She likes Harleys, the Minnesota Vikings, dancing, country music, and yoga. Her sweetest dream is to become a grandmother someday.

For information about Susan Erling Martinez's other books and booklets, please visit her web site: www.tjsusan.com. TJ and Susan are pictured below.